ZEINAB,

THE FEBRUARY

TRIUMPH

THANK YOU FOR YOUR

WONDERFUL ENERGY ¿

LIFE.

Patricia Fontaine

3/17

The February Triumph

A memoir

By

Patricc Fortiori

NOVELLARTS

NOVELLARTS.COM

The February Triumph

For information address the author P.O. Box 263375

Houston, Texas 77207

www.novellarts.com

First Printed 2015 United States of America

ISBN: 978-0-9963261-9-3 (ebook)

ISBN: 978-0-9963261-2-4 (print)

To Angelica,

Thank you for the long hours of your companionship during both the crisis around us and the one within me as I struggled with my depression. Thank you for sharing your life story, your smile and your tears. Most of all thank you for sharing your heart. You will never be forgotten. I hope that one day life's ocean is small enough that our ships might sail next to each other again. Until then, we have the February Triumph.

To everyone who bravely boarded The Triumph in February 2013.

For

Robin Williams

On February 7, 2013, The Triumph set sail from Galveston, Texas on a short three day tour of the Western Caribbean that turned into an eight day disaster for over 3, 400 people lost at sea. The February Triumph chronicles this life changing event that occurred simultaneously at the height of my battle with depression. The February Triumph is the true story of this struggle through depression and the disaster at sea.

CONTENTS

1   Saturday, March 31, 2012: A set up from the beginning   1

2   Sunday, February 3, 2013: Depression and The Devil's Ride   4

3   Thursday, February 7, 2013: Three days at sea. Bomb Voyage!   10

4   Friday, February 8, 2013: Characters & the cake   25

5   Saturday, February 9, 2013: The calm before the storm.   41

6   Sunday, February 10, 2013: Fire teams to engine room six!   45

    9:15 am Red Bags, White Sheets and Black Nights   66

    Angelica   77

    Mickey Leland World Hunger and......Peace   91

7   Monday, February 11, 2013: Depression takes its grip   101

    11:30 am The Legend   108

    Mahler and The Dabhol   126

8   Tuesday, February 12, 2013: Alcohol & Depression-Bar Brawl   129

9   Wednesday, February 13, 2013: Movie night- fight night!   140

10 Thursday, February 14, 2013: The final push. Stronger.   147

11 Friday, February 15, 2013: Home   155

Saturday, March 31, 2012

A Set Up From the Beginning

Armed men dressed in long black overcoats gathered outside the Galveston Texas harbor boardwalk.

The words 'UNITED STATES MARSHALS', jumped from the back of their coats in large white letters as the group prepared to engage the harbor with an order in hand from the United States District Court. The marshals took guard positions around a gaggle of men and women that included a representative from the United States District Court, a Port of Galveston security officer and a witness, then ushered them through the entrance to terminal 1 where a nearly one mile long, 101 gross tonnage vessel lay moored in the harbor. The group stopped at the dock end of a slim gangway that stretched into the forward section of the ship's port side and conferred amongst themselves verifying the orders of the court. After the short pause they stormed across to the ship, the MS Carnival Triumph.

Once aboard, a Triumph officer accompanied the group to the Captain's Quarters on deck 8 just outside of the bridge.

It was a tense moment as the marshals crowded and secured the room.

The Triumph's captain rose from his high backed soft tan leather chair and was immediately met with these words: "We are here to execute an order of the United States District Court. We are seizing this vessel!"

December 14, 2012

The Triumph experiences mechanical issues and propulsion problems. The ship's sail was shortened and its itinerary changed from Cozumel to Port Progresso only. A specialist is flown in from London, England to Mexico to assess engine conditions and direct repairs. The specialist recommends restricting the Triumph's speed on its return to the Galveston, Texas.

January 2, 2013

Captain Angelo Los receives notice of recommended safety upgrades to the Triumph's fuel distribution systems. In the notice, the deadline for compliance is February 28, 2013.

January 29, 2013

The Triumph experiences propulsion problems and engine power loss. It is forced to abandon its itinerary and return to the Galveston Texas port at less than half speed.

The February Triumph

Sunday, February 3, 2013

Depression and The Devil's Ride

"What are the odds?" I asked myself. "What would be the odds of one day finding a moment of peace in my life, a moment away from the weight of depression that has pursued me for years? What are the odds that after so much time in the darkness of this illness, light could finally get through?" Depression was so heavily upon me I envied John Proctor in bearing a life destroying weight and being able to ask for more to instantly end it all. Could he have carried the weight everyday as I have?

What would be the odds in continuing to find misery and tragedy in a short life ending in an unsatisfying death? Is it just a matter of statistics, or is it a matter of the numbers being right for just one particular person? Will I have a life filled with pits of despair or one with hills of hope? I ran the numbers and this is what I have come up with: In a world of nearly 7 **billion** people approximately five percent of us are at a level of existence that can be described as 'scarcely content'. Far less than that 5 percent, closer to one tenth of one percent, of us can find continual bliss. The greater population of our species is in peril. I am, and most like me are, in complete denial.

I live in a state of over 25 million people and in a city of over 3 million people and I find myself deeply entrenched in the ninety-five percentile fighting each day to live, fighting each day to breath and struggling to experience stability in some way either emotionally, physically, financially or psychologically. I fight depression.

The numbers are overwhelming. Just by the numbers it is possible that no one on this side of the planet has ascended to the less than one percent which means I am surrounded by misery and yet I have pretended it is not there. I was trained to ignore it even though it sits in front of me, watching me and I, it. Even worse, I am sensitive to the depression of others and so their misery is added to my own and thus my depression grows exponentially. Only Jesus could carry this so I needed to reduce the numbers. I needed to reduce the swelling and the pain of misery compiled by my proximity to others.

In short, I needed a vacation.

I needed to escape the ninety-five percent.

I needed to be away from life.

I needed to be far away from life and even further away from my own life.

I needed to be away from a painful break up with my girlfriend, a career stuck in a sink hole and falling through the ground. I needed to be away from a family stricken with a disease of abuse, isolation and separation. My decision to sail the Triumph was not from planning months in advance, it was not from weeks of consideration, nor was it from days of preparation. It was a snap decision a few hours before the ship was to set sail on that fateful Thursday evening, February 7th, 2013.

Since loosing my job in 2008 my income level dropped to less than half of what it once was. Re-climbing the ladder above poverty meant endless rounds of waiting, applications, interviews and denials.   It was a vicious cycle of anticipation, expectation and disappointment.   Combined with a 12 year relationship that was going no where my sanity and morality was constantly under attack. When my depression hit and hit hard I can only describe the experience as *The Devil's Ride*.

After an agonizing weekend of going back and forth with my girlfriend fighting over whether or not to stay together, she finally broke up with me.   After this I could not sleep and   completely lost my appetite.   I was hungry and afraid.   It was indeed the devil's ride with a seat reserved exclusively for me.   Depression is a roller coaster that is continually going round and round up slowly and quickly down.   Nothing is more agonizing than this quick movement, except when the car was still.   My car is a 1971 Imperial plying the streets of Houston, Texas.

Nikki's birthday was Friday, February 8th and in a last ditch effort to save our relationship I grasped at hope with an attempt to win her back by taking that much needed vacation together.

Late Sunday night I toiled over pressing the submit button on the purchase of a cabin.   I waited nearly thirty minutes watching the screen refresh its information, knowing that if I press that submit button my life could take one of two fateful turns.   One, I would spend thousands of dollars on the Triumph and that would sink me even further into insolvency, increasing the depression in my life for a marginal and brief moment of happiness.   Outcome number two was no better.   I would spend another weekend alone and in agony in the devil's ride.   Happiness, as hope is, is always a long shot and the least likely of the outcomes and yet I bet against those numbers and hoped she would go.

I was feeling the crushing weight of reality versus feeling the uplifting strength of a fantasy. The reality is that I was struggling to survive and the fantasy is that I needed to have and possess a real form of love in my life. I needed to escape reality and maybe, just maybe I could find a parcel of stability in my relationship to place a toe upon where happiness and relief from my depression would come thereafter. In those minutes before I decided, I quickly went through the cycles of emptiness, loss of hope and lack of purpose that depression thrust upon me while struggling for basic survival just to make it to the next day. For me, it is also a cycle marked with weariness, anger, hunger and a thirst to be whole.

At 2:15 am Monday morning, 72 hours before the Triumph was to set sail.....I pressed submit. I tendered my soul and the money evaporated from my account. It disappeared as though Scotty himself beamed it off the screen and into the vastness of space. In an instant I was broke.

The next few hours found me deeper in the cycles of depression and sending me on an involuntary food strike. I could barely eat as my favorite foods lost their taste and hunger drove me to the edge. As my body became weaker and weaker I drifted off into light momentary sleeps hoping the dread of watching my savings disappear would soon be gone. It never left. The anxiety of knowing what I had done in spending so much money hung over me during my Monday work day so I stayed after 5pm to make over time. Constantly thinking about loosing the money was pushing towards the doors of the devil's ride; this would be twice in less than 12 hours.

After years of struggling in underemployment, debt, foreclosure and tax liens I had managed to grab a logistics job that allowed me to walk the horizontal line of poverty. The competition for even this job was tight, so missing days meant I could easily be out of a job. I could not advance forward, I wasn't sinking, but I was not moving and to loose time and money on the Triumph would set me back for months. To lessen the blow of my absence from work, I planned to work the Thursday morning of the Triumph's departure and the Monday evening of its return. I stacked everything against the chance to rid myself of my depression if just for a day.

Tuesday February 5, 2013

I hoped the week would pass without incident, but the devil's ride came calling again. On Tuesday morning I was invited to a job interview that I had to attend before Friday. Since the company was located adjacent to Hobby airport, my departure point for Galveston, I chose Thursday morning at 8:00 am.

Over the next two days I fought with my girlfriend over the phone for hours trying to persuade her to go and that maybe things would change with a good vacation and the hopes of a new career looming. She was not convinced.

Thursday, February 7, 2013

Three Days At Sea. Bomb Voyage!

The devil ride knows its role and knows it well. It would not release me from depression without a final jab and a hefty serving of false hope. I was up at 5am looking at the ceiling wondering what this day had in store for me. Wondering where this ride was going to take me.

I packed my bags, put on a suit and started the day with my scheduled interview at 8 am. I didn't expect much from the interview and by this time I had completely dissociated any feelings of hope from the possibility of getting a good job. I was completely and fully desensitized to the interview experience and I had jettisoned optimism long ago.

For the interview, I smiled, asked the questions, feigned interest and engagement, but all along I checked my watch counting down the minutes until the Triumph.

I closely watched my phone for my girlfriend to send me a message that she was on the way or that she was waiting for me at the dock or at the airport. After a promising interview I regained my appetite. The last shuttle from Hobby to Galveston was scheduled to leave at 1pm and I still wanted to log some hours at work. I went in, in my suit and hit the warehouse floor for two hours before heading back to the airport.

As I sat in my car eating lunch, I envisioned receiving the '*Dear Applicant: Thank you for your application to our position but we have chosen a candidate whose background is closer to our needs.*' email at any moment. It did not come; instead I received an email from the manager thanking me for coming in and promising to get back with me early next week. I didn't put much thought into it. I was done, I took the devil's ride and got off close to my stop but not quite there, but the devil has many rides and if I stepped out of this car I could be stepping right into another. I needed that job. I needed to get my life back on track. I felt it contributed to the hole of depression that widened in my soul.

Depression aside, the breakup was taking a heavy toll on me and the vacation would be a new path that would have us reconnect and heal. I hadn't eaten for days and sleep was even harder to come by but I found a moment to enjoy a sandwich and listen to the radio. I went from checking the time every ten minutes in the interview to every five minutes.

In the interim, there was another woman in my life that I waited to hear from. Her name is Terry Gross and everyday at 11am I listened to her on NPR's Fresh Air carried by KUHF. I had never seen her but I loved her voice and how she carried her personality over the air waves. Terry's voice came through to me as sharp yet caring, strong with a vast cultural intellect, and on occasion passionate and compassionate. To me she was just a voice, a woman's voice, a feminine voice that attracted my senses. On this day, she interviewed Bradley Cooper, 'Mr. Sexist Man Alive'. He opened the show with a compliment to her and for the first time I heard Terry excited and almost giddy at having him across the table. She laughed throughout the interview in a way that seemed to give him the show and herself. Maybe it was me, but Terry was a substance person and not one for mere entertainment, so to hear her laugh lightly and softly at Bradley seemed more admiration than indulgence. Every woman who I liked just seemed to get snatched up by another man. And now Bradley, "Mr. Sexist Man Alive" was wooing Terry Gross. Her broadcast always took me away from life for a few minutes so I escaped into the show in an attempt to forget about my girlfriend but instead I listened to Terry lay across the table for Bradley with a pillow talk tone in her voice asking him if he cries like a hyena in real life.

Bradley was there to talk about Silver Linings Playbook based on the novel by the same title. Bradley's characters' name was Pat, my name. Pat fought through depression in a desperate attempt to win back his wife. There was nothing more he wanted in life than to prove to her he was better and that they could make it. I felt a deep connection here. His wife's name was Nikki. My girlfriends name. The connection was too deep. Pat nearly destroyed himself by forcing hope into his life of change. It didn't work and they never got back together. The connection was now too deep.

During the interview I received a text from my girlfriend. "I'm not going!" It said.

Not even Terry could save me from this. The devil's ride was open again and I bought all the tickets. That sinking feeling loomed in the air. I was standing still as the world moved around me, and I was sinking into the depths as the world walked over me like shallow tides rolling in and out. It was a slow and awful death. I was crushed, but a silver lining was burgeoning in that I had a cabin and vacation reserved for me aboard the Triumph.

It is a 50 minute shuttle van ride from Hobby airport to the Galveston and from the shuttle's window I traced Houston's ever winding bayous into the waterways and bays of Galveston. Halfway through the ride I turned my music down and listened to the van speed down the highway. I could feel and hear the rhythmic thumping of the tires over the highways' metal plates. For a moment it took me back several years to the I-10 border run. The Interstate 10 border run was a race five miles before Louisiana's border to Texas and through to Beaumont. It was fun, exciting and reckless, a time when my friends and I would race back from Louisiana and in those last miles just outside of Texas blast through the border. Through the years all of us got caught at some time or another. I could never forget the sound of road vibrating through my car as I picked up speed.

The beating of the tires pulsed through the cabin like drums readying a war beat. "Ba-bump ba-bump, ba-bump ba-bump, ba-bump ba-bump."

I was headed to my destiny.

Galveston's port is truly unremarkable and being lined by a slow and dirty industrial district with scant signs of commerce and small business activity, it is not a huge tourist attraction. On this February day a dull haze stretched across the pier into the brown water and out into the Gulf of Mexico. There is a slight turn in the road leading to the dock and in this curve the Triumph's aft section slowly came into view.

A magnificent ship! From the distance it is a crystal white city that could sail into the clouds as easily as pulling out into the sea. As I approached, the Triumph got bigger and bigger until I reached the dock and could see nothing more the pristine white hull of the ship; the upper decks and the name TRIUMPH along the side.

As the port shrank away into the distance I could feel my world getting smaller and smaller as if I was catapulted towards Elysium with a single and sudden throw. In just a few steps of being on board I was with the less than one percent. Everyone was happy. I didn't need my own music as the ships' party had begun and I could barely hear myself think. The odds were getting better for me as the numbers were getting smaller. I was no longer one in millions drowning by the darkness of their misery and my own. I was now one in a few thousand mostly happy people and being around so many happy people was something completely foreign to me.

I carried my luggage aboard and traced a swatch of passengers walking through the hallways to the elevator. I was engulfed in comfort and luxury. All of the staff smiled. Everyone from the bell hops to the brass shiners smiled and spoke welcoming me to the ship. I was on an island of laughter, lightheartedness, warmth and happiness.

Passengers anxiously crowded the lobby of the deck 3 main elevators overlooking the Capitol Atrium in the forward section of the ship. Some people went up, some people went down. Those heading down smiled as the elevators descended into the ship. Those headed up, as I was, basked in the ascension. Deck 8 is the highest full passenger cabin deck on the Triumph and in its aft section stateroom 83-74 is close to the stairs leading to the patio of deck 9.

A couple on the elevator smiled at me and said. "Don't worry deck 8 is the best deck on the ship!"

Cramped into the elevator, a couple of people got off on each deck and by the time I reached deck 8 only I and three other people remained.

My steward greeted me just outside of stateroom 83-74. He checked me off on a manifest and quickly brought me back to reality asking. "Will Nikki be joining you shortly?"

I sighed, but looked straight into his eyes and said. "No. She is not."

He was extremely polite and sheepishly continued. "Will she join us later before we set sail?"

"No she won't." I said sternly while trying to stay calm.

He scribbled something on the checklist. "Will she join us at our first port of call?"

I ignored him the third time, walked into the room and placed my bags down.

The steward reminded me of one last bit of business before we could depart, saying. "We will have muster in 15 minutes and all guests must attend. You do not have to bring your life jacket but do report to deck 4 section H."

I thanked him and closed the door and suddenly I was alone, completely alone.

I surveyed the room beginning with the closet to the right of the door leading to a small desk and large mirror. Next, a four by four foot painting was over looking a full sized bed on the adjacent wall. A television was hanging over the foot of the bed and that wall connected back to the bathroom across from the closet. I stepped in front of the mirror and took a long look at myself. I was still wearing the suit from the interview earlier that morning. I was tired, very tired and weary from the day and from the week. The suit was also tired after seeing far too many interviews and it was slightly smudged from wearing it to work. I wore it now like an old uncle's favorite funeral suit.

I changed out of the suit and before I could enjoy the privacy of my cabin I was back in the lightly packed hallway and made the walk down to deck 4 via the mid ship stairwell. Gathered in muster area H and barely standing from duress, I joined in the cheer of the families and couples waiting for announcements. There were men and their families, mothers and their teenagers, teenagers and their friends, couples, husbands and wives, little sisters and little brothers, babies and mothers, and then me, by myself.

I stood under the life boats listening to the safety director give emergency instructions and after a few minutes she ended with. "We are a ship at sail and as such the most dangerous condition is a fire aboard the ship so pay special attention to the no smoking areas and properly and completely extinguish all smoking items. Remember, fire is the most dangerous threat to the ship and passengers."

Finally the Triumph was well under way leaving the dingy industrial port of Galveston, Texas haloed by its brown waters behind. I was officially one of 3,142 passengers and 1,086 lovely crew members, a much smaller world.

A quiet sadness befell my heart as we pulled away. Nikki did not come. I was alone. An awful rumbling and emptiness tossed my head, my heart and my stomach. Even as the DJ blasted the rhythms of a never-ending party on the outer decks around the ship I hung along the rails watching the last views of the Galveston port fade away not wanting to ever see it again.

Before we left cell range I called my sister and told her I loved her and that I had made it on board. She made me promise to call her Monday morning when the ship returned. Within minutes there was no land in site and our cell phone signals were gone. I was cut off from the world and in an instant the numbers changed. The numbers of the happy people instantly exploded and the numbers of servile were all but gone. Save one. It was too quick of a change for me. The revelry of the ship, the music, the partying, the dancing, the drinks, the calorie rich sweets was more than I could take in at one time. I needed a long gradual ascension into mollification.

They were enjoying themselves as though a switch was just flipped on, but I was not happy like any of these people. The festive spirit of the embarkation rattled my senses in an unsettling manner exposing my disposition and flushing the deeply held curmudgeon to the surface. So after that brief call I headed back to my cabin to be away from this madness!

A few feet from my cabin door, my steward, Miguel welcomed me back and said. "Dinner is at 8:30 in the Paris ballroom or if you like I can bring dinner to you."

"Thanks, but I think I will go." I told him as I slid my card in the door. Within seconds I tossed my shirt across the chair, dropped in the bed, kicked my shoes off and fell asleep. It was 4:45 pm, Thursday, February 7th, 2013.

Three soft dings came across the intercom as the opening to ship wide announcements began.

With only the small desk light on I laid in the bed with my face down wondering when all of the noise would settle, I wondered when the howling silence of loneliness would set in so I could began to feel comfortable again.

"Ding, ding, ding."

It was Jen, the honored, *brilliant* and *fantastic* voice of revelry, the orchestrator of play, the woman of fun, the leprechaun of happiness, our cruise director. Hearing her voice for the first time raised a brow from deep within my pillow to the point where it turned me over on the bed forcing me to stare at the speaker in the ceiling. Jen

Baxter, at first presentation whipped a heavy tongued British voice with a thick and cheeky UK accent. Her tongued stabbed at the excitement of the cruise and in a true English fashion where make believe was wrapped in a pretty little present and easily sold as reality. Jen was the authentic United Kingdom import, not quite Manchester proper but yet a true gogledd through and through punctuated by her frequently used catch phrases such as '*brilliant*', '*fantastic*' and '*fabulous*'.

After Jen gave some general announcements, the Captain, Angelo Los welcomed everyone aboard. He seemed disinterested in supplementing the festive spirit Jen brought as he talked slowly and stumbled at articulating English through his padded native Tuscan dialect.

Exhausted and completely spent, I fell asleep, but only briefly, as hunger, fear and anxiety all tugged at my vitality. Nikki would have loved the room. It was her style; small, cozy and personal, void of any indulgences and yet stately. Every thought I had of my existence bounced against the Triumph and her. In one second depressed at being there without her and in the next I was depressed at just being there. It was torture. I could not fathom happiness or get into the spirit and as every minute passed I thought less of the vacation and more of being captured by my depression.

Hung high above the bed a 19 inch CRT TV loomed ominously. "I haven't seen one of those in a while." I spoke to my quiet room as I reached for the remote. The top of my head turned from a smoky grey in the reflection of the TV to Tom Cruise scaling a tower.

"Nikki and I saw Mission Impossible together." I said murmuring to myself.

I let the movie play for a few minutes and realized I was too tired to attend the formal dress dinner so I set my alarm to 11pm. Surely by then I would have the energy and enthusiasm to walk the ship and grab a bite to eat.

"Click. Vlooom." The TV was off and as fast as it faded...I did also.

7:40 pm

"Ding, ding, ding"

Jen came back waking me up with the harsher UK side of her voice as she reminded everyone of the first nights dinner.

Still, restless, tired and hungry I grabbed my cabin card. "Dining: Paris, Upper 8:15 P.M. Table: 625." I pulled up my suit and tightened the tie around my neck again for the hundredth time this day and stood in front of the mirror to see a beaten and anguished black man dressed in a tattered suit from a yearlong paper-chase.

"Fuk!" I grabbed my jacket and was out to the upper Paris dining hall, deck 4 aft section of the ship.

Most people dressed for the occasion while some stayed casual. Couples, families and friends were all smiles as they enjoyed the four star service of the crew.   All of the waiters smiled with a courtesy when they stepped out of the way as I was guided to my table.

Along the way, at a table for two, sat a woman who caught my eye, she was by herself and enjoying a glass of wine. A tall dark skinned woman with long black hair. She smiled as I walked by. It was Elle.

The upper Paris dining area forms a U shaped balcony overlooking the main Paris dining hall. At the back of the balcony sat table 625, a table for two, one chair for me and one Nikki.

From that perch I could just get a peek of Elle, but first I had to deal with this continual bit drilling into my head, Nikki.

"Excuse sir." The hostess came over. "My name is Jasmine are you Mr. Fortiori?" Another slim size 1 Asian woman immediately came over to greet me and get my meal started. "Will the misses, Nikki, be joining you this evening?"

"No!" I said with a nonchalant politeness but she continued to finger the trigger.

"Oh, she will join you later after the main course?" Her soft accent and demure stance was impossible to disguise as an assault on my sanity but I withstood it.

"No, she will not." I replied nicely. Now I could feel the devil's ride coming for me as she toyed with setting off my depression.

This one had an itchy trigger finger as she continued. "Oh, is she not feeling well? Would you like me to send a meal to your cabin?"

"No." I said lowering my head and rolling my eyes.

"Will Nikki be joining you for dinner tomorrow?" She kept.

She wouldn't take a hint. "No!" I insisted and flapped my eyes like a broke winged bird trying to fly away. "No!" I grunted again.

The maître'd observed the not so friendly roll of my eyes and came over quickly begging. "Hello Mr. Fortiori, is there a problem?"

Before I could answer Jasmine placed me in the car, stepped one leg in pressing the gas and said. "Oh, he is here by himself and is dining alone."

The waiter quickly looked at the roster pulling Jasmine away and slammed the door on me. "Will Nikki be joining you tonight?"

I rolled my head and wrenched my neck in agony throwing my hands up like a bomb had exploded. "No! Again, NO! Not tonight, not tomorrow night or any other night or day! No! No! No!"

He pulled away, turned Jasmine aside, spoke to her in private and snapped his finger signaling the support staff and pointed to my table. The support staff swarmed my table and the setting across from me was gone. I sat their looking at the empty space brightened by a spotlight from the ceiling.

"Poof!"

"Here you go sir, so you'll remember this moment." The ship's photographer popped by with an antique disguised digital camera.

That sinking feeling hit me again. There was always a moment on the devil's ride when I realized I was a helpless passenger chained to my depression. The ride forced me to experience all the pain and anguish around me and left me incapable of fighting it or responding. It rippled into my eyes, my ears, my nose, my mouth and my thoughts taking a course through my central nervous system to my heart where it built to implosion. All I could do was feel it. An incalculable amount of time passed as I sat stunned in place staring at the emptiness across from me. I heard nothing, I saw nothing and as the room filled with hundreds of people there was only one man at a table for two, me. I was hungry, angry and afraid.

Once the spell subsided, I came back to reality and looked up for Elle. She was gone. "Great." I sighed and threw my napkin on the table.

I ate everything twice over and ordered more while everyone else was noticeably conservative. Women picked at small pieces of fruit on a saucer and cut small steaks into cubes that were smaller than the fruit squares.

"Is anyone hungry?" I asked myself watching them float around with tiny plates and big smiles. I couldn't understand why they did not eat when so much food was everywhere.

It was just too happy everywhere and I did not fit in and with Elle gone, I lost the will to hang around and enjoy the ambiance. By 8:45 I took the long route back to my cabin and toured more of decks 4 and 5.

I saw Elle again at the casino; she smiled as she passed. My heart was deep in despair and my body not far behind so I could not come up with the energy to say hello. I watched her walk away moving between the black jack and poker table and then out of site. As she faded away, so did my energy so I cut my tour short and took the rear stairs up to the Lido deck, deck 9, just above my cabin. It was crowded with people in line for a small slice of pizza, a quick drink or a snack.

Again felling the rush of exhaustion I grabbed a slice of pizza, collected three drinks from the bar, a bowl of fruit, a stack of cakes and took the short drop and turn down the stairs back to my cabin. In my short absence Miguel tidied the room leaving the *FUNTIMES* for the next day, fresh towels in the shape of a parrot and chocolate squares in the center of the tightly wrapped and perfectly aligned bed. After a quick shower I was back in bed. Finally, this day, February 7th, the longest day of my life, was over.

Friday, February 8, 2013

Characters & The Cake

With an insulated door completely sealed from the interior of the ship, there was little noise and no light so I slept solidly and peacefully. Opening my eyes to the dark room I had no idea of how much time passed. Feeling refreshed I wanted to just stay in bed and so I did but quickly my thoughts turned to how short and lonely this weekend would be if I did. Sleep was my anti-depression defense and so when I got a good long sleep I always felt better. It was already Friday and we were due back Monday morning so after one night of sleep the vacation was nearly half way over and 10 hours had passed.

After a few lingering minutes I pulled the FunTimes agenda close to my face. My eyes kept drifting up to the date on top of the page. Friday, February 8, 2013. It was Nikki's birthday. No matter how much I read through the activities list for the day, the date kept popping into each sentence. It was haunting my intellect and as I tried to purge it from my pupils by diving deeper into the page, my eyes would roll back to the top and see Friday, February 8, 2013.

Friday was billed as a fun day at sea and there were a few events I wanted to attend. The Park West art auction was on the list. Park West has a reputation for supporting national and international modern artist including my favorite, the astounding brilliance and genius of Marcus Glenn. At 1pm in the Oxford Lounge, deck 4 aft, I placed a check aside the Live Champagne Art Auction. I placed another check by the time for 3:45pm in the Rome Lounge, deck 3 forward, the jackpot bingo. I also wanted to get some time in on the black jack and poker tables. As I perused the 2 page colorful layout again my eyes kept floating to the top of the page to the date, Friday, February 8, 2013.

Morning was almost over. I was hungry again and decided on a light breakfast so I slid into my sneakers, made a left out my door, took the short 50 foot walk down the hall, another left into the stairwell, up half a flight and I came out under the outdoor canopy of the rear of deck 9 in seconds. Instantly, I could smell the warmth and clean air of the open sea, my throat and lungs felt like a freshly popped bottle of champagne bursting with the light and life of the sun. I stopped to feel the radiance and took several deep breathes.

"This is healthy." I said. It was naturally wholesome and good, unlike anything I had could remember experiencing. I felt an invigoration of energy, peace and calmness. Next, the jazzy good morning thrive of a gas grill captured my nostrils. In this robust thrashing of my senses was fresh eggs, bacon, grits, ham, biscuits, hash, chorizo, flour tortillas, pancakes, waffles, sliced pears, peaches, chocolate milk, croissants, butter, pork, toast, grape jam and oatmeal just feet away from my door and I wanted to eat it all. The few early risers gathered in small groups of two or three at a table talking softly fingering a cup of coffee or tea. I took the scenic route around the Lido deck to feel more of the morning sunshine and see the ocean. It was beautiful, blue and empty. I was surprised to see a basketball court and an outdoor track circling above the ship. "In time." I told myself "In time." I put running the track and shooting basketball on the list.

For now, I wanted food. I was still hungry. I fell into the breakfast buffet line with an appetite of a hungry lion and stared down the polished steel trough with an eye to take it all away in a trolley. It was gluttony but I was well ready to step up to the line and look over to the other side, but before I did, I surveyed more of my fellow early morning risers. To my surprise I could not understand why they were taking the small plates and selecting one or two items and just picking at a few things as they went through the line. I grabbed the big plate, two big plates, no three big plates and two bowls and pushed forward stacking on a carton of chocolate milk and another one bitten between my teeth.   At the end of the line I struggled to lift the tray and in doing so I looked up and saw Elle watching me frozen in disbelief. I didn't care. Depression made me a cynic and for me I could point a finger right back at everyone else and label them accordingly, so back into the stairwell behind the stacked tray I went, and after the quick one left and two rights I was back in my cabin.

It was Friday, February 8, 2013, Nikki's birthday and I was in my cabin alone stretching my stomach beyond its natural capacity. Hunger was a trigger for my depression so eating kept the fall into depression at bay. "How could they pass up such a meal?" I choked reading over the FunTimes again while stuffing my face.

As my agenda for the day crept up, a good night's sleep and the food were beginning to impart a hint of levity even though I was still uncomfortable around people. Mixed with the vibrant rays of the sun, glitzy popping of the casino and extraordinary cleanliness of the ship, the beautiful colors of the inside of Triumph partially eroded my cynical disdain for contact with other people. Exactly what activities would I let them pull me into I did not know, but I suspected I would not enjoy them either way.

Triumph's interior is reminiscent of a hotel casino lobby. It is walled by shops, venues and store fronts carved into decks 3 through 5. A quick ride in the capitol elevators gave me an enchanting tableau styled view of the ship's mall with passengers staged inside and outside of the venues. Stopping just behind the Oxford Bar and dance floor I registered for the art auction showing in the elevator's lobby on deck 3 and then took a walk forward to the gift shop. It was Nikki's birthday and I know she likes rum so I bought a bottle of Captain Morgan's from under the 'get it while it is duty free selection'. In line at the register, I took a moment to stop and watch the people behind me and those walking about in the shop. They took in the merriment, the lights were bright, the windows were crystal clear and the chrome accents of the shop glowed majestically. A wave of depression whipped across me raising the hairs on my neck and blurring my vision. I was spending money I didn't have and for what?

Turning back to the line in front of me I noticed Krusty, the Ukrainian clerk, eyeballing me before he spoke. "Ah yes. We have special deal for you. Buy two bottles, enter drawing in 30 minutes and if your cabin is called your bottles are free!" He said with a Russian accent.

One for me and one for her I thought and so I said to him. "Okay. I'll take two then."

"Yuri! Another bottle for the gentleman, he's feeling lucky today." He yelled to his comrade working the floor.

Yuri came over with a smile put his arm around me and said: "My friend, the Smirnoff is buy one large bottle and get the smaller free. It is the best deal on the ship and promises to give plenty of memories and pleasure to share."

"No, I think that's enough." I told him and with that purchase the only money on my card was gone.

Krusty swiped the card and gave me a receipt. "Don't forget to come back for the drawing in 30 minutes, because you could be our lucky winner!" He followed.

In my estimation I tendered my soul twice and bought three tickets reserving a seat on the devil's ride in less than five minutes. One ticket for buying Nikki a bottle, one ticket for spending my money on it and another ticket for even thinking I could win and of coarse the remembrance memento, a receipt. That is how my depression works; it sabotages any good feelings I could expect. It forces me to build a tinder house of the most combustible incendiary material around and then it sends me into it with a torch.

The man's enthusiasm was too Krusty The Klown ridiculous for me to bear so I fought back showing my cynical side and took back to the mall and window shopped along the stores. I made the circuit around deck 5 visiting the sidewalk bodegas filled with unheard of fancy named watches, jewelry, wallets and purses. In the center of the mall lobby, a set of spiral stairwells curved from deck 5 back down to deck 3 and hooked into slim walkways aside the Oxford cigar bar.   Everything shined, glistened, sparkled and was spectacular. I took the port side and turned forward past an empty library corner and through to the 'internet café'. The Triumph was fitted with special transmitters, a satellite based communications array, for passengers to access cellular signals and the internet. There was solace in knowing so many people chose to be away from the world and weaned themselves from the connections to the misery of those whom they are connected to.   Instead everyone partied, danced and drank.

Most of the crew of the Triumph originated from countries outside of North America making the occasional American a standout, and there were no greater American standouts than the members assigned to the art auction. The auction was led by an American of the likes of a Mob Boss Jimmie Fallon and he was assisted by beautiful strong arming woman, a *'Jessica Eye'* of New Jersey that had the build and attitude to match.   Together they considered themselves part of the '*Americans*' and after a day at sea, I noticed a very considerable difference between the attitudes and personalities of the American crew members versus those from the Far East. According to their tags, accents, names and physical features most of the crew came from eastern hemisphere. Malaysia, Cambodia, Thailand, Indonesia, South Vietnam with the remaining hailing from further north in India, Nepal and some of the former soviet satellite states and some as far south as South Africa. No matter where they were from these crew members provided an environment of service, pleasure and comfort unparalleled in normal American life. They totted a big smile with bright white teeth, happiness at serving and courtesy was the moniker under which they spent every second. It was genuine, refreshing and continuous amongst them all. Their smiles lasted long after their mouths were closed.   Their programmed indoctrination at delightful service was so deep it lightly lifted them from the sublime background of a beautiful ship. A lifting so subtle they were softly two-dimensional, like pop up cut outs in a children's book.

Against this, the American's were 'real'. They carried a privilege amongst them that presented itself as a muffled disdain toward service. Jimmie and Jessica could not fake it. For the very few of the crew that was American, in just a short moment after their smile disappeared, the air of arrogance was apparent. They were not comfortable with selling themselves and less comfortable with selling themselves as a happy product for other pleasure seeking Americans.

Norton Chasing Ali

At the entrance to the art hall, just outside of the internet café one item caught my eye, a print of Norton Chasing Ali was on display. I had seen another photo in the series years ago and it became the iconic image of 1973 showcasing the physique and intelligence of Mohammad Ali. Norton, who broke Ali's jaw in the fight, posed with the champ for several shots in Yankee stadium. In this shot, Ali feigned tipping away on the soft green grounds of Yankee stadium as Ken Norton playfully reached out to him from behind trying to tag him. I loved it and I wanted it. I placed a blind bid on it and piece by Marcus Glenn.

Back through the internet café I passed the shops again and joined a small crowd gathered in the lobby of the gift shop. Krusty pulled up a small step stool and began to pull receipts. I've never won anything in my life but standing alone there in the midst of all the other happy and cheery people I felt hope. I decided to wait knowing that after the first or second pull I would be on my way empty handed. There is something about my depression that makes me want to confirm the misery I feel. That's how my depression kept my ass in line.

The crowd gave only a second for a winner to step forward before they pushed, 'PULL ONE MORE! PULL ONE MORE!'

Krusty was getting frustrated because by now he called six cabin numbers, and then finally. "83-74!" He yelled.

I was stunned.

"83-74!" he yelled again.

My eyes popped to life. "Here! Right here!" I waded through the crowd holding my cabin card high above everyone's head.

Krusty looked at the card. "Yah mai yo!" He screamed. "You're the winner! Ladies and gentlemen a round of applause."

I smiled and nearly cried. I felt like a homeless man hitting the lottery after giving his last dollar to the church. Everyone was happy for me. They smiled. They cheered. I felt warm and embarrassed at the same time.

"Just one question!" Krusty interrupted with his Russian accent. "Do you want to double your money back or double your liquor back?"

Two old women, two grandmas, Patty and Selma, holding hands bumped up close to me. Patty rubbed her elbow into my side and whispered with a smile. "If you get the liquor we can drink it up in our cabin."

I stepped a bit closer so only Krusty could hear me. "I'll double my money back."

The ladies winked at me in unison. I walked away.

For just a few footsteps, a few seconds I wasn't drowning.

I could breath, but only for a moment.

By the time I reached my cabin that good feeling was gone. It evaporated into the depths of my depression and misery at being alone. No one was where I was. No one was in this mess of a life. On this ride I was alone. No man takes a cruise alone and I felt I was the only single man on the ship.

I contemplated whether or not I should attend the art auction. I picked up the 'FunTimes' and again focused on the date, February 8, 2013, Nikki's birthday. I looked for a way out of going as very reason to stay in my cabin floated around me until something unexpected happened. Krusty made me smile.

I attended the art auction and Jessica was as forceful as she was beautiful reigning in a disdain for being an American peddling art at sea better than anyone ever could.   With Jimmie, they had a near Chicago style gangster intimidation to getting the bids they wanted. They bruised and prodded anyone who flinched or raised a brow at any piece, even the giveaways. Jessica's seething evil was of wicked witch of the west proportions, but with the beauty of Cinderella.

There among them, a softer and kinder blonde South African dabo girl catered to the crowd. "Up, up, up, up!" She stirred between us. "Up, up, up, up!" She danced through the crowd pointing to bid cards and tapping others that sat in the hands of anxious players. "Up, up, up, up!" She pleaded to get our bid cards in the air. "Up, up, up, up!" She tickled, teased and poked at us like show ponies. "Up, up, up, up!"

The tension was high. The intimidation was rough and callous to everyone.

I loved it!

Jessica and Jimmie whipped over the crowd with an authority and skill at getting a number that would make even the staunchest of used car salesman proud. I liked seeing other people uncomfortable and under pressure and the addition of the dabo girl was the perfect fit. It felt welcoming to me, it felt like home but after three hours of this torture even I had had enough!

It was six-o'clock, so I scuttled back to my cabin with several plates of desserts and waited.

I waited.

I waited and stuffed my face with sweets.

I waited for a decision on whether or not I would try the formal dinner again. I felt confident the staff would be aware that I was dining alone and another Nikki fiasco would not occur.

At 7:42 p.m. I decided to go because I needed another full meal.

Again, Elle was there. I walked past her, smiled and continued to my table, 625. The hostess and wait staff acknowledged me and smiled as they always do. I stared across the table to the other setting hopeful they had the new plan.

Finally, I could have that promised elegant and refined dinner for one and a moment to enjoy it. I had the suit on again and was sipping from my wine glass when a woman from a neighboring table came over and asked for the chair across from me to add to her table. I smiled and happily relinquished it. She took a moment to sit down at my table and make some small chat as her friends shuffled around to make room for her.

And then it happened.

"Surprise! Happy Birthday Nikki!" The wait staff and hostess rushed over a small round white cake. "Happy birthday to you! Happy birthday to you!" Several of them broke out singing as they placed the cake in front of the woman sitting across from me.

'Happy Birthday' was written into the round white cake with a gold anchored toy ship pushed on its side.

The woman was stunned and mortified thinking she had stolen the spotlight.

I was in complete disbelief. It could not get any worst, until.

"Let's have the lovely couple get together for a picture." The pirate photographer swooped in and angled to get her in a shot with me.

The woman slapped her hand against the table. "I am so sorry! I didn't know." She tried to tell me.

"Just take the fucking the picture!" I pushed through gnashing teeth feigning a smile.

As fast as the camera clicked she popped up and grabbed the back of the chair sliding it passed me.

"Take this too!" I dropped the cake into the chair.

Seconds later another troop of staff turned the corner looked at me sitting at an empty table and focused on the lady with the cake next me and crowded her table and let out a big "Happy Birthday Nikki!" and started singing again.

"I can't believe this." I dropped my head in my chest.

I had enough and every ounce of my sanity was gone. I quickly downed three glasses of wine and when a young waiter passed by I tugged at his apron. "Is that your table upfront?" I asked him pointing to Elle sitting alone.

"Ah, it is and a fine young and single lady she is." He smiled knowing my intention. "I'll ask her if she'd like your company sir."

"No, no...wait." I took his pen and scribbled a note to Elle.

He took it over, she read it and scribbled something and sent the note back.

"The lady seems interested sir, he smiled. I'll help you out, I've only seen her with an older woman, maybe her mother." He said.

"Maybe next time." The note read.

I stared across the audience to Elle as she sipped at her glass. I was ravenously angry and couldn't compose myself to a decent conversation and at that point wanted to just get straight to it, so I stood up and scribbled a response. "I don't think I'm coming back, but you can call me at 83-74." I wrote.

The waiter ferried the note over. Elle unfolded it and I looked away to avoid an uncomfortable glance. When she turned back, I was gone.

I ordered the full meal, all the sides and all the deserts and told the waiter to have it delivered to my room.

I was drunk and stumbled through the ship with a sickness that nauseated me. It was the devil's ride again. It was a dizzying and horrid walk as a tightly controlled violence boiled inside me. I had to let it off.

I went to the small Monaco casino mid ship on deck five in the hopes to stock up on cheap drinks and get a little black jack in. Friday night was warm, jumping and lively and I hoped that warmth could defer my thoughts away from taking a P90 to that cake and the wait staff. This trip for hope had turned into my personal corner of misery. Apparently, my depression not only owned a car but it also had ship and its name was Triumph.

On the Promenade, deck 5, I grabbed a seat at the black jack table. The players were not serious and were dropping money as fast as the waitress dropped cheap drinks. I had another one and then two more from the bar just outside of the casino area. The drinks were coming faster than my play.

Another drink came to me before I finished the third. "I think you are delivering these to the wrong person." I told the waitress.

She smiled, nodded over to a far corner and said. "No, I'm not."

It was Patty and Selma.   They smiled and gleamed at me acknowledging the gifts they sent over.

The old women turned my stomach and reminded me that I wanted to be alone so I left the casino and continued forward on deck 5 to the Rome lounge balcony. The show production billed as a musical 'Wonderful World' had just begun.

It wasn't Broadway. It wasn't off Broadway; it was off off off off Broadway but invigorating. The cast meshed together spectacular samplings from Chicago, Phantom of the Opera, Beauty and the Beast, Lion King and Cats.

A jovial and cheerful audience rewarded the performers with a long round of applause after each major musical. The show was capped off by ticker tape explosions and West Side Story's 'I Want To Live in America'. The performers came from all corners of the European

Union and blended spectacularly onstage. I applauded them and realized that I was an American and remembered the context in which Bernstein penned the words.   Here I was, an American, at sea, where vacation voyages were symbolically reserved for the privileged and elite and yet depression and unhappiness plagued my life. And them on stage, the working and struggling for life, happy at the prospects of pursuing their dreams while dreaming an even larger dream, of being American.

I was ready now. From the moment my shuttle beat rapidly down the highway to Galveston I was determined to try to turn this time into something positive. I had work to do.

At 11:45 I made it back to 83-74 and I relaxed in the bed with my stomach bursting and eyes rolling from the dinner and drinks I pulled in.   As before, Miguel left the new 'FunTimes' with the Saturday, February 9, 2013 date on the desk.   I read it thoroughly to make sure I made it to midnight. "Finally." I said, and I the lyrics of a song came to my mind:

> 'Well I know, I miss more than hit!,
>
> With a face that was launched to sink!,
>
> And I seldom feel, the bright relief
>
> It's been the worst day since yesterday,   yes
>
> It's been the worst day since yesterday.'

All I could feel was a headache and in a few more seconds I felt nothing.

Saturday, February 9, 2013

The Calm Before The Storm

Sleep became my second best friend in the past two night's right behind my best friend, food. They kept me from spiraling into a depressed state. I had another good night's sleep that was only broken by the leprechaun voiced director Jen Baxter who gave a brief summary of Cozumel. From my bed, wrapped tightly in thick sheets I reviewed the shore excursions and seriously contemplated going ashore, but first I had another stop. Cabin bathrooms are by no means spectacular, a hydraulically controlled toilet, shower and single basin contained in a room the size of a walk in closet. I needed the toilet and a refreshing shower. After eating so much over the past two days a bowling ball sized explosion of my frustrations was ready for release. A toilet and a shower. We often take for granted the importance of these seemingly minor provisions in our life knowing we can live for short periods of time on limited water supplies for drinking, however that life quickly turns to hell without a toilet and a shower.

This would be the last bath I would have for six days.

Breakfast was the next order of business. Again, I slid into my sneakers, made a left out my door, took a short 50 foot walk down the hall then another left into the stairwell and up half a flight of stairs emerging under deck 9's outdoor canopy.

There were only a few people on the deck and fewer in line as most of the passengers disembarked in Cozumel. The port was crowded with ships from several different companies. The Triumph docked between two other large vessels. I spied the shore and Cozumel surroundings from the railings of deck 10. The Cozumel beach near the dock was confined but the local streets were bustling with businesses and tourism. The ships provided the thousands of tourists that hit the stores along the boardwalk collecting shopping bags and little trinkets along the way. At just one deck below the highest deck on the ship I was so high the people looked like ants scurrying away from the great white mounds of the ships.

I did not want to loose ground on working so I jumped into the breakfast line and started stacking my plate. This time I noticed snickering from other passengers watching me collect food as I moved along. They had lightly weighed saucers of fruit or slices of toast, so they looked at me with disgust and reproach. I sneered back.

To them it was fashionable to appear frugal and ignoring the necessity for food. It was *'pretty'* to be seen as light, free and wanting for nothing to eat. If they took in a big plate, they only picked at it and left more than half of it on the plate to be discarded. I cleared all my plates and yet they scoffed at me. I was hungry and they didn't know what hunger was and how it affects my depression. Hunger magnifies my depression and the depression intensifies my hunger. So as they looked I grabbed and when I grabbed and they looked. They sneered, I grabbed more. I grabbed more, they sneered. By the end of the line the plates stacked up to my chin and I started the balancing act down to 83-74.

After a big breakfast I took a short nap and at 1 p.m. shoved the stack of empty plates outside of my door and went up to the port side of the upper South Beach Club lounge on deck 10. The location was just out of the way of most traffic and was the perfect spot for seclusion and concentration.

I resolved to try to make this a working vacation. All the food I can eat, all the alcohol I can drink and uninterrupted sleep awaited me, and I needed it all.

I wanted to write and many months had passed since I had an opportunity and the concentration to do it.

My working vacation was to compile and review all the notes from my outlines and to fix a nagging technical problem. My notes were spread across three devices and two back ups. All of which I brought with me along with an extensive list of music I had not gotten around to enjoying. So with a nice supply of Earl Grey, hot water just a feet away and a restroom in the corner, I pulled up to a small table close to the wall against the inside window of the balcony and started.

I tuned out the entire surroundings of the ship and started my playlist with Antonin Dvorak.

By 4 pm passengers started to trickle back. An hour or so later we were under way again. I stopped briefly and stood up from my chair to watch the sun go down. A sunset was on list but I wanted to save that event until the last day which was just over twenty-four hours away.

Saturday night was party night and the celebrations where everywhere on the ship. The dance floors were filled, the pizza line stayed busy, the bars were bustling with people and every chair of every casino table supported a warm and intoxicated body. At 9 pm, I hit the buffet below to stretch my legs and add to the pile of dishware steadily accumulating around my table. My private little section of the deck 10 balcony was empty so I stayed there for the night.

Passengers flirted in the hallways, couples necked on the balcony, teenagers laughed, skipped, ran and pushed at each other all over the ship as younger kids ran, hopped, jumped and played. The mood was festive, fun, happy and playful but as the night got later and later the inhabitants quickly left the kingdom of goodness and started to slowly ply themselves to the golden calf. Women skipped around half naked, drunk with all sorts and descriptions of body parts hanging out for other men to grab and fondle. Men skipped around half naked, drunk with all sorts and descriptions of body parts hanging out for other men to grab and fondle. By midnight I reached symphony number nine and felt a whisper of peace. Music is also a buffer and relief to my depression.

Sunday, February 10, 2013

Fire Teams To Engine Room Six!

At 3:30 am on Sunday morning after more than 15 hours at the table, I was done. My eyes could not stay open. My brain was drained and my intellect was exhausted so I gathered my setting and left.

When I arrived at my cabin, Miguel had again made up the room leaving Sunday's *FunTimes*, more chocolates and a note from guest services on my pillow. In the past 15 hours I had not a thought about Nikki at all and here, before the experience could escape, guest services wanted to know if I would pay a 15% gratuity for her portion of the reservation. I was tired, dog tired, but this poke at me required an immediate response so I turned right around and headed to guest services.

It was after the long Saturday night of fun so the ship was sparsely populated. By this time, everyone was drunk and passed out. Some people stumbled along to their cabins, a few sat around the piano bar but most of the halls where empty.

At the capital elevators the doors opened to a bright and sparkly kid depressing the deck 10 button. "Hey, you stopped me!" He complained.

"I'm going to guest services, deck 4." I told him.

"Guest services is on deck 3." He whined. "So I guess we have to go back down." He said and pressed the button for deck 3.

"What are you doing in here?" I asked him.

"I'm just riding the elevator up and down. From deck 10 down to deck 1 and back up to deck 10 again. The pool is closed and there are no movies on so I'm just riding up and down." He sung.

I couldn't believe it so I had to ask: "How old are you?"

"Six." He said.

"It's 4 in the morning. You should be in bed."

"I know." He said. "My mom and dad went to a party so I'm going to just ride the elevator. Here we go, deck 3, watch your step someone threw up just outside the doors."

Guest services allowed me to waive the 15% for Nikki. Apparently, they also did not know she was not aboard.

Snafu aside, I was redeemed. I had written more in the last 15 hours than in the last 6 months and realized I nearly allowed my dreams and passions to be wiped away behind my depression and a relationship that devoured my mind and undermined my spirit.

I set my alarm for 11am. It was Sunday and we were due back in Galveston in 24 hours and regardless of all the people and what was going on around me at the time, I was alone.

In the darkness of my cabin the ship seemed unusually still and quiet. I raised my eyes to the ceiling and before I closed them I whispered. "I need more time."

I didn't immediately fall asleep. My eyes just lulled for a few seconds tracing the dull khaki ceiling wanting more than just another day.

4:07 am.

"Ding, ding, ding."..

My eyes moved over to the speaker in the ceiling.

Jen came on and there was a hurried pulse I her voice. "Good early morning everyone. I just wanted to inform everyone that we do have a situation going on. There is no immediate danger but we do want everyone to know we have a small situation at this time and we will keep you informed."

"Ding."

4:15 am

"Ding, ding, ding." The speaker vibrated as if the bridge was kicking at the mic.

Jen again. "This is an update to the announcement a few minutes ago. We do have a situation onboard and many people are asking questions. We have the situation under control and are looking to getting you more information as soon as possible."

"Ding."

I wasn't too worried because a situation could mean anything, a brawl in the casino, a fight in the bar or someone fell down a flight of stairs. It was a situation I didn't have to worry about it and I was nearly asleep.

4:30 am

"Ding, ding, .ding."

"This is Jen again." Her hurried pulse went a tone higher and it was clear she was rushed in filtering her information.   "We do have a situation on board and many people are asking questions. Some of you are gathering in the muster areas with your life jackets and asking about releasing the life boats. We do not need you to do that. We do have a situation onboard and we will keep you informed."

"Ding."

"SHIT! WHAT THE FUCK IS GOING ON!" I shouted jumping from the bed quickly. "SITUATION!! What the hell is a SITUATION?!" As I got closer to my cabin door I could hear a rabble increasing from the hallway and a faint and tart smell eked in the air.

I opened the door to a hallway clogged with people in life jackets squeezing and pushing to get by in both directions. They pushed at each other so furiously trying to pass and jockey for position that some of them fell into my cabin.

A thick plume of smoke and soot plummeted up the hallway from the forward section smothering everyone in its pathway and instantly caused a symphony of coughing and choking. The billow found my now opened door and grabbed me by the neck singing my sinuses, throat and lungs. The taste and burn of the particles was obvious as an industrial fuel, oil, plastics and metal. A salty, metallic and acrid assault punched at my senses leaving me breathless and burning from the inside out.

In response to the smoke, the current of the crowded hallway changed; everyone turned to the aft stairwells at the back of the ship, but they were stuck and clotted by their life jackets. From inside my cabin I could see the horror and fear on their faces as the stampede shoved and climbed over each other like rats fleeing a sinking ship. A sinking ship! My slim doorway was a horrid portrait of passengers being stomped on by climbing over each other in terror.

"Shit!" I didn't know what to grab first but I couldn't breathe so I grabbed a towel and gagged my nose and mouth. My eyes burned and I knew I had only seconds to get out of the cabin!

I tossed the room around not knowing where my life jacket was. I fumbled around holding my breath and was quickly loosing my sight but I had enough time to find a pair of jeans and sneakers, no socks.

At the door I looked for a space to jump in the crowd and wondered if I should I try to run down four decks to the life boats or take the short walk aft to the top deck. I decided on the upper deck.

4:35am

"Ding, ding, ding."

"Everyone we have situation on board and some of you want to launch the life rafts. Again, we do not need you to do that, but if you choose you may remain in your cabin or go to the outer areas of......"

Jen's announcement was cut short by an authoritative male voice:

"Fire teams to engine room six!

Fire teams to engine room six!"

This announcement was immediately preceded by the voice of the chief engineer Nunzio Priolo. "Alpha teams to engine room six! Alpha teams to engine room six! Alpha teams report!"

A powerful and dangerous fire blazed in engine room 6!

With seconds left to hold my breath, I dived into the sea of life jackets stuffing the hallway and pushed into the pack while fighting to close my door. The usual quick few steps to the corner stairs took forever. I couldn't see more than a foot in front of me as the life jackets bricked the hallway sealing everyone together. Everyone had a life jacket, everyone except for me.

I couldn't hold my breath for much longer and just as I thought I would give way to suffocation, my section of the crowd burst onto the Lido deck under the pool canopy. The crowd scattered in all directions as I took the center stairwell to the outside of deck 10. My table was still leaned against the window with an empty cup surrounded by torn bags of tea and sugar.

When I left the deck 10 little more than a hand full of people walked the ship. Now, several hundred spread across the outer parts of deck 9 and 10.

A thick black smoke popped from the center exhaust vents of the ship.

Another man stood close to me watching the spectacle and said. "I've been out here for awhile and I noticed we stopped moving about 30 minutes ago."

"Is it bad?" I asked him.

"If they are lying to us like this, it's bad. Take a look on the side." He pointed to the side of the ship. Smoke was pumping out of the side of the ship.

"Smells like fuel." I said.

"Now." He said pointing to the center stack that was also puffing. "Imagine how much fuel it takes to get a ship of this size and weight back to port. If the engine room is on fire this ship is a floating BOM....."

"BOOM!"

Before he could finish his sentence, a huge explosion rocked the ship. It felt like a bomb exploded in the mid section.

The explosion rattled the wooden deck plates and shimmed across the metal rails. The lounge chairs shuffled, danced and tapped across the deck. The vibration jimmied my legs as a huge puff of smoke belched from the center exhaust stack and out from the sides of the ship.

The Triumph moaned in agony like an injured whale grasping for air. People began to scream as the ship snapped and rattled uncontrollably. The Triumph started a pitch to the starboard side threatening tipping over into the sea.

Panic broke out! Men, women and children screamed for their lives and ran the incline from the starboard side of the ship to the port side.

Screams and yells pierced through the dark and pungent air:

"It's going turn over!"

"It's going to sink!"

"We're going down!"

"We're all going to die!"

"We need to get to deck four to the lifeboats!"

Chaos raged across the deck as men loosened their belts and tied themselves to their family members and some tied themselves to the railings of the ship.

One man tossed the patio furniture overboard and screamed. "We'll need something to grab on to!"

A woman and her children huddled, put their hands together and started to pray. "Our Father in the Heavens hallowed be thy name.."

From the rear of deck 10 I saw the random confusion of hundreds of people scattering in the dark in all directions terrified the Triumph would capsize or burn down to her hull.

A couple hugged each other through their life jackets saying their last words. "THIS IS IT!" She whimpered. "I love you."

The man said nothing.

The Triumph continued to toss, pop and rattle.

Random screams grew in number and intensity as it was clear there was a huge explosion and fire and the ship was a smoking inferno. My instinct was to run, but there was no where to go. There was no land, no shore, no beach, no sand or dirt to put a foot on.

Afraid myself, I could barely move, so I stayed still. I was stunned that this might be it. I was in shock and in my eyes and ears I captured the last moments of a sinking ship and a doomed people. My heart sped up and beat furiously as this was yet another occasion I sat at deaths door. Yes, I had been here before; something was too familiar about this feeling of being so close to death, it felt like the depression every day of my life increased one hundred fold. Something about seeing people run for their lives and the rise of water was eerily familiar to me. It frightened me to the core. I had been here before and it scared me because I knew the feeling of being helplessly trapped while waiting for a slow death. I had been dealing with that fear for years and now in an instant I saw and felt it in a palatable form that drove my depression.

"This can't be it! This can't be it!" I panicked thrusting a fist down to my side.   The Triumph shook, rattled and popped more.   I officially lost it as the muscles in the back of my neck tightened. "Shit. I think this it." I whispered to myself.

People ran around me in a madd fury, bumping into each other and knocking into me.

The Triumph tossed about a bit more and then all the lights went out!

In an instant, everyone on the ship disappeared.

The ship disappeared and all I could hear were the screams and howls of the night. The people across the deck and the frame of the ship vanished; the man and woman a few feet away from me were erased into the darkness!

Only the stars gave light and only they could be seen. The dark and calm sea became the sky and the sky became the sea as they were one.

I was still too afraid to move. The small parcel of wood on which I stood floated freely in space far into the cosmos. I could no longer tell the water from the sky; I could not tell the reflection of the starlight below from the starlight above. I was afraid that if I took one step I would walk right into the heavens.

If I could give myself over to it, it would be beautiful, free and spiritual as if I was softly gliding through the vast open emptiness of space lit by stars in every direction.

Was I dead? Was I in the milliseconds before death where my neurons pounded away their last spikes of life overwhelming my brain and flooding it with every memory and imagination of my consciousness? I didn't know for sure, but if I was going to die and if angels lived this way I wanted to be with them and I wanted to be in that moment forever, freely traveling through the stars. Those minutes lasted a lifetime so I didn't move. I didn't want to loose my place, I didn't want to look back, I didn't want to look down, I didn't want to look to the side so I stayed focused straight up into the stars. My depression wasn't suicidal, but I was ready to freely give myself over without a fight.

As quickly as the stars came they were suddenly gone and my wings were clipped as I realized my feet were anchored to a burning ship, the Triumph. Sounds of the Triumph grabbed my legs and brought me back to life. An exit sign nearby flickered, popped, fizzled, went out and came back on.

A hushed calmness breezed over the deck as we all, waited, watched and listened.

Everyone was quiet as we waited, watched and listened.

We waited, watched and listened.

Movement around the ship became less random as people gathered their senses and pulled into groups calming themselves but still not sure if we were out of danger. A steady stream of unspent fuel laden black smoke continued to pump from mid ship and the upper exhaust pylon, spewing several yards away from the pristine white of the ship only to settle back and cling to the hull.

More than a thousand passengers and crew came outside to decks 9, 10 and 11 as the rest stood along the walks of deck 4 and 5.

I know the devil's ride very well and on this ride it was always accompanied by a dubious communiqué.

6:05 am

"Ding, ding, ding."

Jen announced Captain Angelo Los.

The captain, with a thick and heavy Tuscan accent, chopped through his English in a short but cryptic message.

"Good morning everyone. We ,eh, had a situation in the engine room, one of the sections of the engine room. Now ,eh, my team is checking everything and, eh, we are very sorry about the wake up call so early, but everything is under control and um we have to wait a few hours to make sure that the all the instruments in the system is working properly. So there is no reason for, eh, panicking. I repeat everything is under control and eh I will keep you posted. Thank you so much."

"Ding."

This was not heaven. It was hell and Jen started a pattern of being the bearer of bad news while trying to disguise it as support and information.

I didn't believe Jen and the captain's input made it worst. I waited for an immediate follow-up message to come but none came. The captain left us there to figure it out. The Triumph lost all propulsion and steering, main power was out, emergency back up generator power was out, the buoyancy control systems were out, communications was out, the hydraulics for the plumbing system was out and the fresh water system had become contaminated. The ship was dead at sea and so were we and they had no plan for this.

Far to the east a tinge of light traced the horizontal plane. The sun was rising. Watching a sun rise was on the list, but not like this.

I hadn't slept or rested in nearly 20 hours and this panic tapped my remaining energy sending a surge of anxiety through me. For someone in my state I knew I couldn't last long like this. I tried to go back to my cabin but the hallway bulk head doors were closed sealing that section of deck 8 off from the ship. I took the long way around but without power the soot and smoke could not vacate the enclosed areas. My cabin and its hallway was uninhabitable.

The hydraulically controlled plumbing system and the lack of ventilation within the ship posed a great problem and immediate threat to everyone's health and safety. Without the hydraulic system the toilets could not flush and combined with the malfunction in the buoyancy system, pressure from the listing ship caused most of the toilets to reverse. As I waited for the smoke to vacate my cabin the toilet and sink overflowed. Fortunate to be on one of the highest decks with no cabins above me, I only had to deal with sealing off my bathroom. On the decks below, sewage immediately began to seep through the walls from the decks above.

The floors became soaked with piss and shit as waste bubbled in the cabins from within the walls. Passenger areas below deck 6 were a toxic environmental hazard and health danger. Sporadic areas in the aft sections of decks 8 to 11 were only marginally better. In either case, staying in the cabins was impossible, so the masses began their journey top side. For all practical purposes, the Triumph was wrecked at sea with the outdoor decks becoming a small cramped island of refuge.

Holding my breath and gagged, I tried my cabin again at 8:30 am.

I passed a trickling of men in the hallway as they warned me about suffocating if I stayed to long. My room was pitch dark with no light from inside and no light from the hallway so I used the light from my phone to guide may passage into the cave. The air was still and deadly with a turbid stiffness.

The letter from guest services was on the floor. That 15% saved me. If I had not taken the trip to deck 3 hours before I would have fallen into a deep sleep like the night before and because I was alone, I would have suffocated to death. I was unprepared for that moment and just stared at the paper remembering how my depression fueled anger drove me down to deck three and I thought it might have been better if I had not. I had yet another remembrance.

I stuffed my small shoulder bag with a few essentials and headed back up to fresh air.

"Ding, ding, ding."

"Good morning everyone, this is Jen again and I'm here with a few updates. As many of you may know by know we have had a fire in one of our engine rooms. The fire teams responded quickly and **brilliantly** I might add and the fire has been contained. A bit of good news there. We are currently waiting for the temperature to go down in the engine room so we can send the guys in and assess the damage and I'll get those assessments back to you as soon as possible. We would also like to ask that if there is anyone that is need of medical attention that you let a crew member know as quickly as possible. That would be **brilliant**. We have been informed that eh um power is out around the ship and our engineering crews are working around the clock and as fast as they can go to get power restored. In the meantime the outdoor buffet on the Lido is open for breakfast as well as the service lines around the ship. One last time, we are out of danger and will update everyone as information becomes available. You may either make your way back to your cabins at this time or visit for a few moments on the outer decks."

"Ding."

The breakfast lines were long, longer than I had ever seen them. No power meant no grill, no grill meant no cooking, no cooking meant no meat, no hot water, no oatmeal, no scrambled eggs, no hot sausage and pancakes. With a smile, the staff dolled out a seemingly unending amount of cold cut fruit, veggies, bread, milk, juice, sweets and boxed cereal. I passed on it all.

I checked my phone, I had 67 % power and it was draining fast. The power count down was on as anxiety and tensions continued to rise, but I was feeling the worst was behind me until another dubious communiqué.

"Ding, ding, ding."

Jen with her thick British accent was back. "Hello again everyone. I am back to give a few status updates. As mentioned earlier we are still waiting for the temperature to go down in the engine room. The crews are standing by and we look to have an update soon. Umm, we have been in contact with our home office and they have released a statement to the press and public and your families letting them know our situation. A special hotline for your family members has been set up so they can call and receive updates on your status and we are giving that to them as we go along. Main power is still out and as some of you may have noticed the ship is slightly listing but we are um completely safe and in no danger. Fortunately it is a beautiful, warm and sunny morning and the weather is cooperating **brilliantly**. Many of you have begun to settle in the outer areas of the ship. And in just a few minutes I am going to pop out to the Lido deck and make sure spirits stay high. I'll update you again soon."

"Ding."

"Bollucks!"

I still didn't believe her and neither did anyone else. With every announcement she became less a prim and proper Brit and more of a fat, harsh and coarse deep throated Manchester bar maid. It was clear they were keeping information from us.

Not having a place to go to, passengers endlessly roamed the decks trying to grasp the situation. They stirred amongst and around each other dissolving their anxiety in the cauldron of others. It was a completely different scene from the day before. There was no music, no dancing, no drinking, no happy faces, no joyous cell phone calls and most of all, -courtesy had been extinguished. Passengers, who shuffled from line to line and from table to table looked for a place to settle, grumbled and avoided eye contact. When there was eye contact it was blank and dark. I took post at the top of the center stairwell overlooking the Lido deck to watch the masses come out from the smoke filled ship.

Elle entered the spiral stairwell and made her way up to talk to me. "Did you get any sleep? I saw you sitting at that table all night. I passed by several times but you never noticed me. What were doing?" She asked.

"Just work." I said.

"What I would do for some work right now." She said pulling her hair into a pony tail. "There is nothing to do on this ship and I can't go back to my cabin."

"I am out of mine also and the bulk head doors are still closed. They close those doors to delay fire, smoke and water movement from section to section. Now the fucking doors are holding the smoke in. You're here with your mom right or is that your mother-in-law?" I asked her.

Elle smiled back and respected my gentle status question and said. "Oh that's not my mother, she's a co-worker. We won tickets for the Triumph, if you call this winning."

"Where is she now?" I asked.

"Some where. I don't know. She's old, not in the best of health and with the fire we have no where to go." We are on one of the lower decks and it's really bad down there. I can't get in to change clothes or check on our stuff." Elle said.

"My cabin is about 50 feet from that door." I pointed across the Lido deck. "It's on the inside with no balcony no window. Normally it takes just a few seconds to get from there to here, but when the chaos started it took me nearly a minute. Good thing is I am here alone so it's just me to worry about."

Elle was quiet as we watched the scene across the ship then said. "83-74, I remember. You don't seem to be worried too much and what type of man goes on a cruise by himself? At first I thought that woman with the cake was with you, but it looked like a mix up. It was quite funny actually. Hopefully you didn't ruin her birthday."

I parted my hands, smiled, bit my lip and avoided an answer.

"How long do you think we will be like this?" Elle asked me.

"I don't know. Jen said the fire destroyed the engine room and they will not know how bad it is until the repair teams get inside. Until then we can only wait and hope for the best." I said.

Elle took a few minutes and surveyed the deck. "There are more people coming out. I think the entire ship is outside. Do you think anyone got hurt in the fire or died?"

"I heard there was a broken leg, a lot of bumps, bruises and inhalation issues. Suffocation is not a pleasant experience and this fuel based smoke and soot does not go away easily. I could only take it for a couple of minutes." I said.

Elle held her phone up for a signal. She got nothing. In a frustration she pushed it back into her pocket and grabbed the sides of her head. "I don't believe this!"

Deep inside I felt the same way; in fact I was in far worst condition than she was, but I was more experienced at hiding it. No, not more experienced, better trained into submission by my depression. I was on edge, but kept it tightly sealed within me. Something about being a man made me push my depression down, so deep within me that I denied it existed and I would deny I couldn't control it.

Elle's eyes filled with tears. My depression would never allow me to cry from just thinking about myself. This type of self imposed dissociation was critical in denying myself remorse. For my depression to control me, I could never be a victim that expressed feelings. I could only sit there and feel the pain. A victim is human, has motions and an existence. As a victim I could feel sorry for myself. I had to be an object, an object that would cry for others and not for myself. I could only watch as the pressure built in Elle so I offered her a distraction. "Do you play dominoes?" I asked her.

"What?!" She said.

"Dominoes. You know dominoes." I said.

"You brought dominoes on the ship?" Elle said in disbelief through her tears.

"Yes, I did. They were by my bag when I was packing so I just threw them in. My best friend and I play a lot so I am always looking for a challenge."

Elle shook her head, took a long stare at me and brandished a strained smile and said. "I love dominos."

I smiled back and we pushed away from the rail and headed over to the table where I sat the entire night. The balcony tables were quickly filling up. Passengers brought pillows and sheets to the tables creating makeshift beds in the booths. Many bought their mattresses and settled on the floor between the tables and on the outside of the deck.

"I can't believe you brought dominoes. This is so cool." She said laughing.

I told her. "Fair warning, I am good at this. Don't let me beat you too bad."

Elle laughed and said. "Fair warning to you sir. I am very good at this and you ain't said nothing but a word mister, and don't let me beat *you* too bad."

It was good to see someone smile over the disaster we were in. Elle and I tried to ignore the continuing frustration that surrounded us as we retold our stories of where we were when the fire broke out.

We talked over the game which was a good diversion and truthfully Elle was good, real good.

"I'm from Oklahoma and I work for Coca-Cola. We had a drawing for tickets and I got lucky. If this is lucky." She said again musing. After sometime and getting a little more comfortable with me, Elle told me she was married and had a kid.

There was always distress in here voice. "I – I invited him to come but our schedules were not right." She choked as her emotions started to resurface. "I miss them and I know they are worrying about me and I don't want them to worry about me or be scared about where I am." Elle fluttered and started to cry again.

She put her hands down on the table and sobbed. For Elle to be so tender in emotion and yet such a formidable woman dug into me. An athletically built black woman, tall, long black hair, perfect fit and trim as Elle was, she softly gave way. The cracking of her voice, slight tremble in her fingers and tears scratched at my heart. She missed her family and she knew they missed her. No one missed me.

I handed her a napkin to wipe her face and tried to divert her feelings away from the ship until:

9:15 am Red Bags, White Sheets and Black Nights

"Ding, ding, ding."

"Hello everyone this is Jen again with a few updates. I just wanted to let everyone know that the fire is out and we are still waiting for the teams to get inside and make an assessment of the damage. We are in contact with our home office and they have notified us that they will be rerouting one of our sister ships, the Elation to come by and resupply us and they should be here by approximately 2 pm. Once we have an assessment of the damage we will inform everyone on when we will be back under way. However, very important information folks on the, em, toilet system here on board. As you probably know by now the toilets are not flushing and its going to start posing a little bit of a problem in a short while. So we've come up with a plan. So folks what we're gonna do is we're gonna deliver some red bags to all of the bathrooms on board including the stateroom bathrooms, your cabin bathrooms and if you do need to do a number two we ask that you please do deposit that into the red bags and then we're gonna put metal bins in the corridors on every deck on the ship and if you will be so kind as to drop them into the metal bins in the corridors that will be fantastic. And if you do need to do a number one, everybody to save filling up the toilet bowels if you can do it in the a..um shower that will be brilliant! I know it's not the best scenario folks but it seems like the best option that we have right now. So once again we're gonna deliver some red bags to your cabins to the bathrooms and if you can if you need to do a you know a number two, if you need to poop, please do it in the red bag and drop it off in the bins in the corridor. And if you need to do a number one, that's a wee, please do it in the shower. Thank you folks and I'll be back with any more updated info."

"Ding."

Even Jen seemed stunned and surprised by the details of the announcement and having to dispense the news and the bags.

Elle started to break. She leaned over the table to whisper to me. "I hear we are running out of food. Is that true?" She asked me.

"I hope not. If I get hungry it might get a little ugly around here." I said.

Elle looked around and noticed people bringing plates of food up from the buffet below.

"I'll get us something." I offered. As I walked away from the table two disturbing events fell upon on. One, people were bringing up very very large plates of food but the choices were all the same; boxes of cereal, yogurt, apples, oranges and bananas. Most had croissant bread sandwiches stuffed with mayonnaise, mustard, ketchup and sliced onions. Second, and after Jen's timely announcement I felt a rumbling and tussle deep inside my colon. After eating so much over the past day the first order of business was coming with a fury!

The lines for food were long and only offered a few picked over fruits, bread and cereal. I grabbed two plates and headed back to Elle but by then her spin into the reality had taken a firm grip.

"Are you okay?" I asked her dropping the plates down.

"I just can't, I just can't!" She whimpered and cried dropping her head into her hands.

"Can't what?" I asked.

"I have to go." With that Elle pushed away from the table and ran off.

The pressure had overcome her and it was getting to me. I light sweat broke across my forehead. I wanted to eat but my system was so compacted I couldn't force another swallow down.

We spent two hours together and I thought I made a friend and now she was gone. The only friend I had, gone. I could feel the depression coming back. Loneliness is a powerful trigger and weapon for my depression.

It wasn't my fault, it wasn't her fault. There was only one person to blame for this.

"Ding, ding, ding."

"Hello again everyone, this is Jen. We just wanted to update you on a few things. First, our damage assessment teams are still standing by to get into the engine room. We do have a report on the status of the ship. Power is still out on all decks. This means there is no ventilation in the cabins. Our crews were successful in getting a few toilets working on the port side of the ship in the open passenger areas. That's great news. We now have a loo."

The rest of the message faded in the background as I realized why I broke the light sweat. I gathered up the dominoes and made a mad dash around deck 10 to the port side forcibly holding in the massive load I accumulated.

First I tried the restroom tucked between the buffets.   It was flooded.

Squeezing my ass as much I could I fumbled down the stairs to the restrooms just outside of the deck 9 elevators. They were closed off and inaccessible.

Running through the ship I dropped down to deck 7 but there was no relief to be found there.

I had only one option, my cabin, but it was still caulked tight with smoke and soot.

Ready to explode, I pushed passed the half open bulk head doors on deck 8 and whirled past my neighbors in the hallway.

At my door I took off my shirt and tied it closely around my nose and mouth. The gag was so tight sweat tickled at the back of my throat. I had three minutes at the most to hold my breath, do my business and get out.

"3........,2........, 1." I zipped my card in the door and fumbled my way in.

There in the dark I sat and in just a few seconds I heaved off what felt like half of my body weight and it kept coming.

Thirty seconds passed and without the suction of the shallow commode I could feel the pile rising nearing close to the rim! I held my breathe as much as I could but I was forced to let out a wisp of air and a windfall pushed back causing my throat to burn and my lungs to choke.   Shit, piss, soot and fuel nearly took me to unconsciousness. I franticly pressed the flush button embedded in the wall to no avail.   Finally, I could take no more and after dispensing as much as I could and nearing to the point of passing out, I forced myself from the plastic toilet, out of the stall and back into the cabin. With barely a decent wipe, I made for the door and fumbled back into the hallway.   Ass sore, choking, with veins popping out of my skull I joined a line of men and women charging their way through the hallway to and from their cabins like gasping miners deep inside a dark black coal mountain.   They were also veiled in gags, ass sore, choking and red.

Finally, back out on the deck with some fresh air to breathe I rinsed my hands with water poured from a small drinking bottle. Afterwards with hours of music at my side I walked the ship searching for some form of refuge or a spot to sit, somewhere to rest my feet, knees and back.

The mood and demeanor of my fellow passengers had taken a sharp turn for the worst. The lines for food were long everywhere and now people took away large stacks of food on two, three or four plates at a time. Those same people who earlier walked around smiling with tid-bits and small parcels of food just a day before now ran franticly back to huddled groups with piles upon piles of food. Worry and panic set in as people were fully frustrated and worried about running out of food. In lines that they would quickly whisk through and grab an item or two the day before now saw hundreds of people waiting three hours to pile their plates as high as they could.   I stood off to the side watching this spectacle of pushing, shoving, frowns, threats and cursing as everyone grumbled and mean mugged each other.   I observed benevolent human nature turn evil right in front of me. A strange feeling coursed inside of me as they quickly lost composure of themselves and spread anxiety from one to another like a pathogenic virus. An artificially created emotional pandemic burned in and around the ship after less than a day in this condition. I had been living this way for years so I felt comforted. Misery loves company and I had not elevated to their level. They were down at my level! Depression drove a fleet of cars like taxi cabs on a busy Manhattan street and every body fought to get in one.

I walked the line from beginning to end watching the worried, frustrated, angry and anxious. Half of the ship searched and waited for food while the other half set up house on the outer areas of decks 4, 5, 9, 10 and 11.

I took the stairs in the aft portion of the ship down to deck 4 through to the casino and back around to the stores that were now closed. On deck 4, cabin furniture accumulated in the walkways. Mattresses, coffee tables, desks, pillows and suitcases lined the boardwalk as the realization came that we had to live on the outside of the ship.   Frustrations built as nerves were frayed and communication off of the ship was not possible. We were dead on the water and cut off from the world.

It was confirmed as permanent failures; we would not get power back, or communications, or the buoyancy system to steady the ship, or propulsion or plumbing and there was no one of a clear conscience to tell us the truth. An irate madness around the ship spread faster than the smell of the piss and shit.

Our only blessing was the beauty of the day and the night. The day was sunny, warm and the still deep blue sea was calm with mild winds and a clear sky cradled the Triumph keeping her steady in the water with an occasionally gentle bobbing. The weather cooperated excellently giving a good season to set up tents on the outer decks and using the sheets was more for privacy than warmth.

By 5pm Sunday the Triumph was a tent covered refugee city. Just under the entrance to the slide on deck 11, the highest point on the ship, I surveyed the shanty town watching the sheets flap in the wind and flat waters just beyond. Looking closely between the seams of the sheets a stream of heads trickled while anxious bodies roamed. There was something familiar about this; something was familiar about the white sheets and the people dressed in white that irritated my depression but I could not put my finger on it. It was buried so deep within me I denied it existed and that I could not control it, but I wasn't sure what it was.

On deck 9 and 10 food lines continued to grow longer. The number of frustrated and scared passengers grew as they continued to pile their plates higher and higher with still fewer and fewer choices. A day before, a femme maigre, picked at small pieces of fruit on a saucer and now that same thin woman balanced more weight on her plates than on her own frame. The lines changed from a day before when men pulled away with light meals; now, they also loaded their plates. In less than 24 hours the Triumph turned from a place where food was the last thought, to a destination where food and water was the number one item of concern. While wondering whether or not there was enough food to go around we worried if we would see another meal or if we would starve. Hysteria and panic erupted with greater frequency in many areas as people isolated themselves and pushing and shoving took over.

With the plumbing failure, food supplies dwindling and morale in a downward spiral, another comfort from a day before fled, power. Devices began to fail. The hunt for power was on and I was hunting also. The constant and deafening smell of shit and piss put me off the fight for food, but not having power to bring my music to my ears inhibited my ability to stay rational and sane so we ripped up carpet, tore through fascia wall paneling's and pulled back floor boards in search for a live outlet but we came up with nothing.

The Triumph was constructed in 1999 by Fincantieri, at the shipyards of Monfalcone in the Italian Province of Gorizia, which meant most of the power receptacles were European with a few of the kind used in the United States. All were dead, with one exception. The ATM machines required a constant power source to recharge their batteries. Ironically, the machines were wired directly into the emergency battery power grid, which only the bridge had limited access to. So in search of power, over went the machines as we spliced into their lifeline for the trickling power supply. Around the ship, lines formed at machine locations for people to charge their devices looking for diversions in digital game play, e-books, videos and music.

My walk through the ship brought me to the bar at the rear of the Club Rio Lounge on deck 5, the Promenade. At the bar several people gathered around and waited for openings on a series of piggy backed power strips.

Dutch spoke first. "Welcome to the power strip café." He said with a kind smile. "We've only been open for a few hours but I think business will be booming.... soon."

"I'm surprised more people don't know about this." I said to him.

Dutch, a big kind man from the Clear Lake area just South of Houston smiled and responded. "We make everyone swear not to say anything and since the bar isn't open no one travels this way."

The patiently waiting small crowd sat on bar stools but no one was behind the bar, so I tossed over a chair and opened my laptop on the sink.

The Aggie Lawyer leaned over and said to me. "You still have to wait in line, but if you man the bar we might let you in early." She whispered pointing to the handles on the liquor lockers.

I winked at her and tugged on the handles. They were locked. I tugged again and rattled them with a bit of strength and then I tugged at all of them again, and a third time.

"Is there nothing back there? Dutch and I were the first ones here since this morning, but I have to get something to eat and DRINK." She said brandishing a Texas A & M shirt.

Though they were not related Dutch and the Aggie Lawyer agreed to leave me in charge while they went up for food and an unending supply of canned sodas. Being the only person behind the bar, I turned on my laptop, opened the top and let the screen glow at me. I had power and it was wonderful. I could listen to music and write and although I hadn't slept in over 24 hours I picked up where I was earlier that morning.

While Dutch and the Aggie Lawyer were out, the Sistas, visited. They were two sisters from Houston, both between 22 and 26 years old and by themselves on the ship. Each totted the latest versions of the iphone that never left their hands, but after a few hours they checked them less and less.

The younger sat on the bar and held her phone up toward the window. "Still no signal." She said. "Is there anyone getting through on this ship?" She asked me.

"No. Not that I know of. I think that we are just too far out." I said. "My suggestion, power up and enjoy what you can."

They both stayed, even after their phones were charged and contributed to the ongoing and alternating playlist of music. We all listened to the stories of others as everyone re-visited where they were that morning. We exchanged what we knew but no one had any real answers.

True to the code, no one put the word out we had power and only the occasional passerby who stumbled upon our spot discovered we perched the best spot on the ship. We had a view of the ocean through the back window, a slight draft from the exterior doors and comfortable seats in open area.

I discovered four large cans of beer and three bottles of the cheap champagne hidden under the sink. "We have drinks now!"

"Hooray!" and whistles came from the crowd.

I lined up shot glasses on the bar and pushed one to everyone that stepped up.

An old woman smiled at me and grabbed a glass.

I poured them all a drink and just as quickly as I held up the bottles they were gone. At last call, everyone looked around to each other raised their hands in a cheer to each other. A spark of life was in the bar. It was the happiest place on the ship. I saved the last shot glass of champagne for myself and after everyone else had theirs I quietly raised it and knocked it back. There was something about my depression that made me highly functional in other people's depression. The more they fought to deal with a dead ship, the better I felt, so cheers to them coming down to my level.

I settled back onto my stool behind the bar dumping my head into the screen determined to get through my classical list. I picked up with Gustav Mahler symphony's number one through four on repeat rotation. His symphony number one was beautiful and seemed to perfectly score the Triumph's mise–en–scène.

Angelica

A soft voice flowed over the counter. "Do you have any water back there?"

I hadn't looked up and thought it was a ridiculous question and responded. "Water? Who is drinking water when we have ...?"

And there she was, Angelica. The beautiful Angelica.

I was lifted above the bar and gently breezed out of the rear window of the Triumph and floated away high in the sky when my eyes met hers.

I choked some trying to get a response to her. "I don't think I'd trust the water from the tap. I hear it has been contaminated."

Angelica gave a soft smile and teased me saying. "I think if you gave it to me it would be fine."

"I do have a small bottle with me." I went into my bag, broke opened a small bottle of water and pushed it across the counter.

"Is this your last?" She asked taking a long drink from the bottle.

I didn't answer.

She poured half of it back into my glass.

"You don't have to jump the line because it really isn't that long." I said.

"I can wait, but I don't have a charger." Her patience and optimism was unlike anyone else at the bar and the entire time she watched me. She watched my hands, she watched my shoulders, and, she watched my eyes.

"No worries I have one. It will take a little longer but I'll be here." I told her.

Angelica handed her phone over and said. "Soo you don't mind sharing, you know, plugging your thing into my thing? It's always nice to run into a gentleman in such a tense situation. You're here alone, it's almost hard to believe." Angelica's smile caught my attention and her eyes never left my face. Also in her late thirties, she showed no sign of ever ageing any further as her skin stayed soft, supple and tightly layed over cheek bones that rivaled Eva Mendez in there high sharpness and Latina style while donning long dark hair and beautiful light brown eyes.

I hadn't felt my depression as heavily now as I did the day before. Sometimes it was heavy and sometimes it was light, but it was always there except in rare, very rare and short moments that fled as fast as they came. This was one of those moments. A moment I was grabbed up into someone else's world, someone who was not suffering from depression. This moment stayed around for more than that fleeting moment, so I gently slid my laptop to the side and sat on the chrome of the sink. "How's your cabin?" I asked her.

Angelica rolled her eyes. "It's a mess. I have a balcony, but it does not help. It's too hot, stuffy and smells like smoke. It's on deck 6 and there is no pressure on the toilet and the shower is awful. I can't stay in there. What about you?"

"The same. I'm on deck 8 with an inside cabin. They closed the bulk head doors after the fire and now they are stuck half open. I can't stay in there more than a of couple minutes. It smells like an engine burning down to the ground and like yours the air is still thick with fuel and metal burned smoke. It's horrible. I could have died in there."

"Don't say that." Angelica's eyes wondered briefly to the long cloth covers over the windows behind the bar. "Can you open the shades so we can get more light in here?"

As I worked to pull the shades up, the crowd moved over and centered themselves on the bar in front of the windows. Far into the horizon, the Elation was coming into view.

"Well relief is in sight!" Dutch exclaimed. "How many of us do you think they can take on?" He added in jest.

The Aggie lawyer pulled up next to him. She still had some beer in her glass. "We should make them take us all! Yea!" She yelled and the crowd joined in.

"Yea!"

"Yea!"

Angelica smiled at me again and said. "You make people happy. I saw you with the champagne. You like making people happy don't you?"

I came close to her and put my hands on the bar and whispered. "I wish I could."

Her eyes rolled to my left hand. "You're here alone aren't you? No man goes on a ship by himself." She said and folded her hands under chin as if to say 'I'm here alone also.' She didn't have a ring, but she wasn't there alone.   Her adult daughter, Zenaida, accompanied her on the trip.

As the Elation came in closer Angelica and I watched with Mahler playing in the background.   We were nearly alone as everyone had gone to the outer decks to see the Triumph's sister ship bring us supplies.

As the bar crowd dispersed to go outside, the pungent smell of sour urine and shit settled in the bar and quickly brought me to my senses. This reality was quickly followed by a warning shot from our holders.

"Ding, ding, ding."

It was Jen. "And a good afternoon to everyone and as you can see our sister ship the Elation is approaching from our starboard side. They are here to resupply us with fresh food and water. A bit of FABOULOUS news for us and for those of you that are worried about eh..um.. our status on provisions. The Elation will be with us for a few hours as they ferry over supplies via their life boats. We are still waiting for word from our home office on our next move but with our sights on the Elation it seems things are getting better."

"Ding."

I looked at my bag on the floor. With only two small bottles of water I worried how long it would last with 3,000 passengers on the ship. A slight nervousness wafted across my back up into my shoulders and into my neck, but when I looked at Angelica became calm.

"This was supposed to be a coming back together trip for me and my husband, but it just did not work that way." Angelica's poise, soft South American Latina accent, sincere gestures and maturity calmed my drop into depression as she talked. She was a manager of several McDonald's in the Phoenix Arizona area, but that wasn't where her passion was as she told me about her family saying: "My grandfather and father came from South America and started a car repair shop. Over the years the business grew and grew until finally they settled on their niche, classic car restoration. They loved fixing old cars and customizing them, and back then it was so much easier. There were no computers and no electronics. The business went from my grandfather, to my father, an uncle and finally to me. It's my pride and joy."

She leaned over the counter and grabbed her phone and pulled up some pictures of her family. They were pictures of old pictures. The love for her family, her father, mother and grandfather was evident in the way she tilted her head to the side as she swiped the screen. The fade and process of the original pictures stylized them in an antique and memorable fashion. Her young parents stood next to a 1952 Bel-Air. Her mother wore a flower dress that waved in the wind and her father a white dress shirt and khaki pants. She kept a deep reminiscent spell going through her family's history and narrated the location, date and setting for each picture.

Angelica had a wonderful family and I could tell she searched for those simpler days when life made sense and good feelings and happiness was as thick as a Texas sized peanut butter and jelly sandwich; and just as delicious. A man, her father, loved one woman, his wife, and her mother and they loved their children and their family. A good life. She enjoyed those moments.

Angelica was comfortable talking to me, she was always open and honest, and although she had a lot to say as we talked, when she was quiet, she spoke volumes.

I made a friend.

She didn't criticize me nor did she judge me. Angelica wanted to be in that moment with someone she could connect with and that someone was me. We had a pact together and without any words she said: 'I want us to get through this together.' She pointed to my computer and asked. "What is it that you do? Who are you?"

I couldn't deny her request and even depressed while lost at sea a rush fell over me knowing that in just a few minutes I touched her passion and now she touched mine so I said. "I am a writer." And from there I revealed my passion saying:

"What do I do here? I Write.

And how do I live? I live in my contented poverty,

as if a grand lord, I squander

poems and hymns of love.

In my dreams and reveries,

I build castles in the sand,

where in spirit I am a rich man.

Yet sometimes from my safe,

all my gems are stolen by two thieves,

a pair of brown eyes!

And here they entered with you just now.

Now all my past dreams have disappeared.

Beautiful dreams I'd cherished,

immediately vanished without a trace!

But the theft does not wound me deeply,

because, in their space they have

been replaced by sweet hope!

Now you know all about me.

Will you tell me who you are?

Will you say? Please do tell."

Angelica smiled. "About me. I drive a Hummer. My own personal Hummer, the big one. I drive it to work everyday. I like big trucks. Yes, it's a monster but I love it, love it, love it. Can you imagine pulling up to McDonald's in a Hummer? My husband hates it." She took a napkin and blotted away a tear. "It's been a hard and difficult marriage."

"It's not always easy." I said and we exchanged how much love can change.

"I wanted him to come but he found a reason not to." She said.

Angelica opened her heart and continued to pour it across the counter for me to receive in the kindest and gentlest of offerings with a trust I never experienced before. She poured it into my glass and I drank. "I even planned for some intimate time with me before I left, but he pushed me away." She said.

I was stunned. "Maybe he doesn't want to have anymore children." Was the only thing I could find within me to say.

"No. That's not it. We already have a baby boy and I can't have anymore children. It's just supposed to be playground now." She said.

"A playground! Whoo hooo! Cut the grass, oil the swing and paint the slid! I love playgrounds!" I cheered.

Angelica smiled. "You're so sweet." She said. "Would you like to see a picture of him?"

Angelica was high class, moderate in tone and pleasant, a mature Cinderella, so I expected someone similar in style.   Instead, her husband was this over weight, hairy tattooed and pierced oaf of a man. He was hideous!

"I shouldn't have married him and if it was not for our baby boy I probably would not have. He cheated over and over again and I just couldn't move on." She complained.

After a few seconds on the picture she went back to her family and told me how proud she was to have a very old picture of her parents and grandparents. She smiled at them again and gave more details on their storied early days in Arizona. She was proud of the success of her father and her family and felt that that success was in danger in the hands of her husband.

"I don't know what's in my future. He never really appreciated me in his life then we had a baby and got married before we could work out our problems. I wish I could take it all back. He just blows me off. I can't even talk to him like I'm talking to you and it's so nice to have someone to talk to." She said.

I reached in my bag for another bottle of water and pulled a few other items out.

"Oh wow! You have dominoes." She said with some surprise.

"You play, because if you do I have a hard time finding someone to beat me at this." I told her.

"It's my favorite. I love dominoes; my father taught me how to play. Coming up in my family we would play for hours." She said.

"Does he play?" I asked her referring to her husband.

"No, but I am glad that you do. I'm warning you Pat, I'm good at this." She said.

For the second time that day I sat down at a table across from woman doing something I enjoy and she warned me about being good at it.

Darkness fell and the Elation lit up like a Christmas tree gliding around a dark ocean. It hung out of the back window eerily looming as some of the crowd came back to the bar.

"I think it's our turn to go up deck 9." Angelica said.

She needed a little fresh air and I needed to stretch my legs.

At least two thousand people crowded the boardwalks of decks 9 and 10 fully covering the ship. "This is not good, it's getting crowded out here and I'm going to have to find a space out here to live." I said to her.

"Noooo." Angelica said. "We can stay in the bar. It's cool enough in there and not that many people. In a place where there is not much privacy now, we at least can talk to each other there without others hearing."

Most of the deck space was taken as makeshift tents and hammocks made from bed sheets covered the surface of the top three decks and families settled in for the long night. Teenagers roamed in packs immune to the seriousness of our desperation but the adults felt the pressure and were beginning to crack as they worried more about food, water, shelter and where to piss and shit.

All of the crew switched to white tee shirts with big letters 'THE FUN SHIP' on the front. They worked endlessly, picking up cups, plates, saucers, silverware and remains of bread tossed aside by the passengers. The trash overwhelmed them as more and more staff gloved up with trash bags and face masks to deter the smell and a feeble attempt to lessen contamination infection for them, but even behind all the trash picking, crap bag carrying, foul stench and piss soaked carpet and decks, they kept a smile.

Angelica and I perched a spot on the aft rail of deck 10 and watched the colorful lights of the Elation in the distance. Our sister ship circled us from the distance waiting for its last resupply boat to come back. It was a dangerous and scary trip from ship to ship and as darkness fully covered the chasm between our ships. In that canyon a large spot light from the Elation targeted the small boat keeping it well lit. Once they were done the Elation sounded its horn three times in the darkness and her crew yelled to us and we yelled back to them. Within minutes the Elation was gone and the pitch blackness of night covered us again. It was completely dark and we were completely alone.

Angelica and I watched the stars. I told her how much I loved the night sky and how in the night before I escaped the Triumph and wondered into the heavens. I showed her the constellations in the night sky and taking her hand I pointed out the twins, Gemini, and it came to life in her eyes.

"Pat, I think I have an app that has these. It also shows you the brightest point in the sky." She held her phone up and waved it around the deck like a magic wand.

"What does it say?" I asked as she tried to get her bearings.

"Umm.... I don't know. Wait let me see." She turned some, repositioned the device and moved around me.   The arrow continued to point off the ship and just as she felt comforted, the arrow turned and pointed directly at me. "I don't understand this. Don't move!" She took a cautious step backwards careful not to move her hand and curved around me making a slow 180 degree turn putting her back to me then looked out into the ocean. With a perfectly still hand she took a whisper to amazement. "It keeps pointing to you. You are the brightest point in the sky."

I had never felt like the sun or the moon in anyone's life, but for the second night in a row I felt like I was in the stars when she said that.

"Pat, it keeps pointing to you!" She said in amazement.

I covered the screen with my hand. "Put it away. I don't think it will work out here."

My depression always kept me in a state where I could not enjoy the simplest pleasures in life and it caused me to say something stupid and push a good moment away. It was a trained response that was still part of me. Most often it was accompanied by a message.

The dubious communiqué.

"Ding, ding, ding."

It was British Jen again. "Just wanna let you know a few things. We have completed the transfer of the supplies from our sister ship the Elation and she's going to be sailing off shortly. Eh, in the meantime the United States Coast Guard are on their way and they should be in the area at approximately between 2 and 4 a.m. in the morning and they are going to be with us all the way until our arrival into Port Progresso, which, um, will hopefully be on Wednesday morning. Again, we should get the tug boats tomorrow folks at noon and then we'll know a little bit more information about our arrival into Progresso. Once again I just wanna say a *huge huge* thank you to everybody who all have been amazing and **BRILLIANT** and lovely and so patient and a big thank you as I keep saying to all of the very, very hard working staff and crew who have been up since 5 o'clock this morning and our still working and will be working through out the night folks. Now, right now, have a good night's sleep I know it's going to be difficult we do once again apologize for all the inconvenience caused by the fire but have a good night's sleep I'll be back with you about 9 a.m. in the morning for any more updates. Have a great night folks and enjoy the morning."

"Ding".

Angelica put her arm around me and looked into my eyes and said. "I'm going to check on my daughter. I'll meet you back in the bar. Oh, and remember, I'm up two games to one."

I watched her walk away but in just a few feet she disappeared. Instantly I felt the loneliness of the darkness and fatigue was beginning to take its grip on me.

Forced from their cabins by the lingering smoke and the building stench from pools of urine and feces flooding the halls, passengers continued spreading out occupying every lounge chairs, table, booth and walk space. They brought their suitcases, pillows, sheets and other cabin belongings and cordoned off small areas of decks 9, 10 and 11.   Desperate and tired passengers took refuge filling the outdoor running track of deck 11. Some pulled lounge chairs closer to the railings as others backed the lounge chairs against the windows of the Upper South Beach Club as more families poured onto the deck filling the opposite side of the windows. Down below in the open areas of deck 9 hundreds more filled in the lounge chairs surrounding the pool and hot tubs. The 60 foot display screen towered ominously over the open deck's pitch blackness in a night filled with spooky movements of white sheets flapping in the wind as passengers endlessly roamed in white bath robes becoming ghosts floating in and among the sheets.

I dropped back into the last free lounge chair feeling the misery of having seen this scene before, people dressed in white with nowhere to go and the impending death by water just inches away. I couldn't grab the picture from my mind because of my fatigue but it was always there and with the Triumph listing at about seven degrees everything was creepier.

Mickey Leland World Hunger   and   Peace

Jen's end of the day message carried a very serious under tone.   It meant no food or water would be available through the night. The beverage dispensers were dry, the water was off, there were no open buffets and the staff carried only red bags of shit to and from the cabins. On deck three, the Capitol Bar pushed out endless cans of diet Pepsi, Tab and Mountain Dew.

The only way to swim above the tidal wave of depression headed my way was to walk and feel everyone else's misery, so I walked the elevator lobby stairwells down through the ship.   At each deck's stairwell lobby, passengers camped on the floor with their bedding and cabin furniture creating makeshift living rooms, dining rooms and bedrooms. Some did sleep, others just sat up right in disbelief of where they were with their ears and noses plugged staring into space and wondering what was next.

I passed my neighbors on deck 8 who were taking their three young kids up to the outer deck. The father said it was still bad in the hallway and wished me luck. Two of the kids Molly and Chad tugged at my shirt and asked for the chocolate treats the staff would leave. The mother was distraught, red faced and tight lipped. They had been arguing.

On deck 7 more families cramped the elevator lobby and everyone was asking if anyone knew if there was food anywhere on the ship. No one had answers. They held on to empty plates in the hopes something would come available before morning. Empty boxes of dry cereal piled up in every corner alongside banana peels and apple cores. Another smell stemmed through the rising storm of piss soaked carpets. The smell of rotting food whipped through the hallway. Without power, there was no refrigeration and at 18 hours the meat, fish, fruit, vegetables and perishables spoiled faster and worsened the thought of not having food.

A crew member stopped, opened a red bag of someone's shit, picked up a few cereal boxes and half eaten fruit, pushed it down inside and kept going. She smiled passing me on the stairs.

On deck 6, Café New Orleans.

A family set up a mini café with chairs and tables in their elevator lobby of deck 6. The small end tables and stools from the cabins took up little room on the floor and each had a small glass with a flower centered inside it.

They were drinking small bottles of water, playing cards, smiling and chatting. One of the old ladies waved at me with a big southern 'C'mon over and hop a squat' invitation.

"I like this corner of the ship you seemed to have settled in good." I said to the old woman.

The ladies at her table were doing cross word puzzles and Sudoku. She peeked over the rim of her glasses and asked. "Where you from?"

"Houston." I said.

"Whoop! We got another one!" She exclaimed and everyone in the section looked up and smiled.

"Where are ya'll from?" I asked.

"Na'leans." She said crossing out a line on the page and pointing to the tables around her. "Got ninth ward over there, Westbank, Marrero by the bridge down there. You here by yo'self? If you wanna get in on card game you welcome."

"Thanks, but I'm on the hunt for food, some sweets really. Have you seen any of those cookie trays around here?" I asked.

"Child, give dat up. Ain't nothing out there. You from Houston? You know, we were in the Astrodome after Katrina. I ain't never seen so many black people in a fuss about where they were going to sleep or eat or if they were going to make it another day. A lot made it, some didn't. It was mighty strange. Now, I ain't never seen so many white people in a fuss about where they are going to sleep or what they are going to eat or if they are going to make it another day. I never thought I'd see that and I really never thought I'd see it like this. I done took my bus rides in my life time when I went to your city and now they wanna put three thousand of us on buses and send us through Mexico. Well, shit on that!"

"Mama!"

The old lady grimaced and looked at the babies tossing around on a mattress nearby and continued saying. "I'd rather stay on the ship. We made it through Katrina and Rita, and we'll make it through this. Thank ya'll city mighty much for taking us on, but I love New Orleans. If you don't find those sweets you're welcome to come back, and if you do find them bring me back a plain white suga cookie."

That pause in the middle of deck 6 was warm, welcoming and felt like home, but I had to keep moving.

Deck 5 was dark. Even with the windows lining the starboard side's Vienna café none of the starlight from outside helped as families settled under the windows. I paused in front of the Triumph's LED chart and wondered where we were and how far off course the ship was. No one had answers.

I moved on to see that more people had settled in the Club Rio Lounge, sleeping in the booths, under the tables and in the aisles. From the elevator lobby I could see Dutch, The Aggie Lawyer and the Sista's were still at the rear bar. There were still not many people there.

Deck 4 just outside of the Upper Paris Dining Room was popular with the crew. Many of them congregated there before heading to their new quarters – the floors, booths and tables of the dinning hall. I stood at the glass doors of the dining hall to watch hundreds of the crew slowly poke around inside the room shuffling around looking for space. Their white shirts made them look like lab rats stuffed inside of a glass box. Exhausted and labored, few of them moved quickly, many did not move at all and splayed themselves across the tables to sleep.

A volley of crew members charged through the doors and forced their way to the stairs down to deck 3. I followed them to a brawl outside of the galley. Scores of passengers attempted to push aside the crew and press their way into the kitchen area. A riot had broken out and the stairwell between the galley and Main Paris

Dining Room was thick with people choking in the still lingering burnt air and hollering for more food to come out. The crew's line broke as passengers fought passengers, passengers fought the crew, and everyone was pushing and shoving each other.

On the outskirts of the mass, teenagers and women grabbed crates of food, moved them back and then disappeared up the stairs. Arms, elbows and fists whaled in every direction. A woman popped a man in the face for grabbing her crate socking him in the eye. His teenage daughter in turn chopped her in the neck. She let out a near life ending shriek and dropped the crate spilling its contents to the floor. The mass slightly shifted like hyenas fighting over a doe and dived in, devouring the spill, the two women and the man. They squashed me in a paralyzingly tight stampede that waved from side to side.

I was pinned, so I also pushed and shoved in every direction in this mass hysteria, and after several minutes I managed to squeeze to the far side and stumble into the dining hall falling at a another man's feet.

He was stuffing his pockets while eating an apple and said. "We call it *liberating* the food supply. Can you believe it? They were going to dump it. Fuckers!"

The crowd swelled in the lobby and began to grow into the dining hall adding more and more hungry passengers to the quarrel. They screamed, pushed, shoved and argued in a shit filled dungeon swimming in piss. A small cereal box clutched in one hand was ripped away by another person standing by and another and another until the box was shredded on the floor leaving the takers to eat the flakes from their dirty bare hands.

I watched the faces of the hungry, starved, desperate and angry. The fear was contagious and the anxiety it caused was piercing and lethal. Many people just sat around looking as if they were waiting for the end to come, as if it was already over, all except the final moment. A strange euphoria saturated my flesh as I watched the depression within me manifest itself in real life. I was able to see my depression on stage in front of me with my own eyes! It was a freakishly unnatural mania that I was completely familiar with and marked by hunger, fear, loneliness and desperation.

Food. Food. Hunger drove everyone to the edge. Hunger changes a human being and this type of hunger, the type where you don't know when you'll eat again adds to the anxiety and urgency to taste, swallow and replenish your energy. Additionally, knowing that some people will have food and others will not added to the panic. Food, water and shelter. There is a reason why food is always first. Food is the most important and lack of it drives people to desperation. I well know what hunger is; both personally and professionally.

I grew up in a home that six other children passed through and we were definitely on a different level than the parents. They carted away food into their room and locked it away from us. We ate the store shelf brand while they took the sweet cereals into their room. If there was Raisin Bran, they would eat all of the raisins out of the box and then slide the bran out. They had sodas, chips and juice, while we drank water and picked berries from the field behind the house for sweets. When they were gone I would break into their room and 'liberate' the food. Not because I wanted to steal, but because I was hungry.

For several months prior to taking the Triumph I volunteered and worked at the Mickey Leland Center On World Hunger and Peace at Texas Southern University. Coming to know the late great George Thomas "Mickey" Leland shaped how I felt about hunger, what hunger is and what it is not and how hunger affects a person, a family, a community and a country. On his trips to Africa, Mickey Leland took to caring for the families and children of a starving village. He never missed an opportunity to reach out to people starving to death, providing them with food, fresh water, a loving hand or a caring hold. One very young girl he picked up and held in his arms close his chest as any loving parent would. At the moment he held this fragile child, she died, in his arms snuggled close in his chest. Hunger killed her and Mickey could feel her life pass away and as her breathe evaporated from her body it passed through him. From that moment on Mickey Leland fought to end hunger in Africa and around the world. He also knew what hunger is and how it changes the very essence of person as they fight to live under this devastating biological, emotional and psychological change. For me hunger was more than an emptiness, it was a trigger for my depression.

Images of small Ethiopian children beating each other with twigs to grab up small grains of rice that dropped to the ground flooded my mind. Standing amongst Sudanese villages of tens of thousands of the hungry, Mickey Leland knew most of them would not survive and would die of starvation. They died slowly wasting away over weeks and months of not having the proper nourishment. Hunger rots the very essence of a human being from the inside out.   It wasn't until the Triumph that I realized Leland had changed me by helping me to see my weakness. The trigger was hunger, and it triggered depression within me because there was always so much food to share and those with it starved us out just to see us in pain. The pain, which was the depression, was always there but Mickey's wisdom and strength made a change in me especially witnessing the hunger in a real famine.

No plate left from in front of me with food on it.

I would never complain about being hungry.

Watching people argue, push and fight for food after less than 24 hours refocused my attention. I remembered Angelica telling me she would be okay as long as I was there. I focused on not letting the hunger trigger my depression. The piss filled air made me less hungry and the fights irritated my sanity. They were supposed to be down at my level, but they were quickly heading to a place I could not go again.

Back on deck 8, many of the interior cabin doors where open and those who chose to stay slept with their heads in the hallway. The hallway felt more like a cell block than a hotel. My neighbors across the hall kept their door open for me to help bring a breeze through from the balcony. They were a honeymoon couple in their early thirties. He settled into the reality that their honeymoon was awash; she on the other hand, wanted him to do something. They argued so much that they consumed the wisps of fresh air that barely came through their threshold.

"If only they would just shut the hell up!" I grumbled.

The bridge was at the other end of deck 8 and she wanted him to march down there and get answers.

She yelled at him. "We need to know where were going? Are there any phones working on the ship? What are they going to do about all our luggage? What time will we get to Port Progresso? How are we going to get home?"

She screamed the questions drilling them in his head and when she finished she started over again. He said nothing, rather, nothing I could hear.

I laid my head in the doorway looking up at a lit exit sign a few feet away with the thought of tearing it open to get to its power source when little five year old Molly stood over me.

She paused her run, looked down at me, knocked twice at my door and yelled. "Spooky hallway!"

Another sibling popped out of the cabin next to mine, ran to my door, knocked on it twice and yelled "Spooky hallway!" and chased Molly.

Chad ran out next, knocked my door and followed the other two.

The kid's mom and dad peeked out of the hallway. Their mother was looking angered, frustrated and embarrassed as she traced the three down the hallway as their dad stepped out.   They were together. My neighbors across the hall were arguing, but they were together. I was there alone. Everyone had someone except for me. I was alone, another trigger. If I had an issue or complaint I could only register it with myself. As the kids disappeared down the black hallway I could see that car, the devil's ride emerging from the darkness.

"Angelica!"

Monday, February 11, 2013

Depression takes its grip

1:05 a.m.

I waited for a moment in the elevator lobby of deck 5 just outside of Club Rio with a white sheet and pillow under my arm. A few more people settled in the lounge, but it still was not full. From under the large painting of Muhammad Ali I looked past everyone settling in for the night on the floor and to the bar at the very rear of the ship. Dutch and The Aggie Lawyer were still there, and so was Angelica. She sat at the bar over to the side by herself. No one was talking to her and every few seconds she looked around and surveyed the room. She was looking for me, waiting for me to walk up, wanting me to emerge from the darkness and bring her some light.

Everyone was talking about Port Progresso and we were all was still furious about the proposal to ship us across Mexico. Even more, by now no one believed in the confidence of the company to execute any plan competently and we knew we were being lied to but without a phone we were at the Triumph's mercy.

My friend was looking for me and in my heart I was looking for her, but behind me that car was coming up fast and when it pulled up I always got in. I always got in and I could feel it getting closer and closer. I could feel my hands rub across the cheap vinyl interior as I slid over on the bench seat. I could smell its stiff, tight, and moldy insides. It smelled like the Triumph. I was exhausted, completely spent and could barely keep my eyes open. My loneliness fueled my depression pushing me to want to go back to my cabin, gag my face and try to sleep with my head hanging in the hallway. I greeted the oncoming unconsciousness of sleep as a welcome respite from this nightmare, but that was the car and something kept me from letting go and closing my eyes. That something was Angelica.

In one of her looks she caught me standing in the lobby and waved to me. As I waded through the crowd of sleepers she watched every step I made and smiled.

She had been crying and grabbed my hand. "I knew you would come back." She said.

"How did you know?" I asked taking a seat next to her.

"You left your computer. I've been sitting here watching it for you. I left and came back a few times but I knew you would be back. Did you have a chance to eat? Are you hungry?" She asked.

"No. I'm not hungry." I said solidly, as my mind floated back to the rabble on deck 3.

"My daughter is staying the night in our cabin hanging halfway out of the side of the ship. We could squeeze three bodies out the balcony if we all..."

"No, no, no, no way. I will be okay right here." I said.

Angelica kept a smile and said. "I thought you would say that so I will stay here with you and I brought a few things we can share."

"Is Zee okay? You two don't seem to spend a lot of time together." I asked her.

"She's fine. We have not always had the best relationship and with the problems with my husband we haven't always seen eye to eye. He was supposed to come on this trip, not her, so I think she feels I would have preferred him over her, and then there is her life. Not a lot of direction there lately. She's not doing that great in college but I think she can turn it around. Maybe you could talk to her."

It was dark, just a little light from the side exit signs and the stars from the rear window reflected against the wood grain and brass of the bar. At the other end of the bar Dutch noticed Angelica was still holding my hand.

I gave her a napkin to wipe her face and said. "I'm glad she is okay, but I get the feeling that this is not about your daughter."

Angelica's eyes wondered. "It's not. I miss my baby, my baby boy. I keep having these terrible thoughts and it makes me miss him more and more. My family has no way of knowing how I am doing. I wonder if they are worried about me. Do they miss me? I don't know how they are doing either. I can't even talk to them. This is so crazy!" She yelled.

"I understand that." In fact I did not. "I am sure your family is fine. They are probably gathered around the TV waiting to see you and so far we are okay so there is nothing to worry about."

"Thanks." She said digging into in her purse. "I have something here for you, for us."

A lump developed in my throat. She pulled out a small slim box and slid it over to me hidden under her hand. We looked into each others eyes and Angelica smiled. I put my hand over hers and held it.

"I hope you are good at this." She whispered.

It was a pack of cards. We moved to a booth and quietly broke the deck.

The ship was tired, pushed to its limits, burned out and devoid of hope. By 2 a.m. all of the lounge floor and booths were filled with the weary. They packed in side by side and head to toe lining the room like sardines in a can. Dutch, The Aggie Lawyer, Young Tarantino and a few other people around the bar still talked quietly not wanting to wake the others. They were tired, but kept on hoping to stem the wave of sadness passing through us all by keeping awake waiting for the sun to shine and sharing stories.

Angelica was tired also. She pushed the pile of scrambled cards away from her and said. "No, I'm not finished talking. You haven't said that you needed anything or that you want anything. We have been talking for hours and you just sit there listening. Tell me, what's that all about?" She said.

"I enjoy the company." I told her.

"Oh, Mr. Fortiori, so stern, stolid and stiff '*I enjoy the company*'. You're not that good with sharing your feelings are you? Do you ever let them out? Everybody's freaking out around here and you stand there without a complaint and say something that probably nobody on this ship could possible be thinking, '*I enjoy the company*'. Do you feel anything, or you feeling anything now?!"

"I enjoy the company." I said again interrupting her. Angelica was feeling the pressure and as her physical strength fled so did her urge to stay calm.

"You enjoy the company? You enjoy the company but what do you feel? Stop being so closed off. I can see the anger in you or is it fear?" She insisted. "But sometimes when I look at you all I see is a brick wall, a mask of a person, like you are hiding from someone. Or is it something is hiding you. What is it? Stop trying to control it and let it out. Let me help you."

Secretly, she poked at my depression and I wanted to turn my shoulder and look for that car coming up from behind so I avoided her question and looked around the room at people tossing around in their sleep trying to get comfortable. Something strange about the scene of white sheets tossing around in the dark bothered me, but I still couldn't put my finger on it so I said again. "I enjoy the company."

Through blood shot red eyes and frequent stretches Angelica managed to keep a conversation. "What are you feeling?" She begged again grabbing my hand.

"I – I enjoy your company." And as quickly as I let it out, her beautiful eyelids closed and she drifted off for a few seconds and then her eyes opened again and closed.

"Let's go outside." I said to her and gathered the sheets. We took the exterior hull stairwell in the bar to deck 9 and were again lucky to find two empty lounge chairs next to each other on the railings overlooking the ocean and star filled sky behind us.

Angelica's soft exhales rumbled against my chest and made me chuckle as I admired the points of light in the heavens. I pressed my chin deep into the crown of her head and released the faint fragrance of an exotic oil that pierced through my sinuses. I could breathe. I closed my eyes letting a tear plop from the right side of my face, past my cheek, over my lips, onto my chin and into her scalp. The bead unleashed another tiny explosion of more fragrance setting my mind ablaze and then more tears fell.

By chance of this situation and circumstance two like hearted people saw one another. Angelica saw me, most of the time she saw through me and I only saw my depression. The depression made me feel that even with so many people around and Angelica sleeping by my side, I was still alone. I tried to see her, but I could not see myself. In a place where no one saw me, she did, and now if I could only look down and see, I would see her thunderously snoring against my chest.

The Triumph listed and bobbed aimlessly without power against a dark night. The darkness was eerie and created a black veil of silence around the ship. The reverie of the ship from two days ago was gone relenting to sheets flapping in the wind against a calm ocean breeze. There was no laughter, no loud shouts of joy, no DJ screaming across the speakers and no music. A gentle refreshing breeze softly steamed through the chairs lightly flagging the sheets pushing the rancid smell of piss and shit over the rails and far out into the ocean reinvigorating the horrifying truth that we were at risk. With no power, no buoyancy system, no propulsion the Triumph could easily succumb to a tall wave from the ocean or sudden shift in the balance of the ship. Ships adrift under these conditions with an incompetent crew do not survive for long. A year earlier, the Costa Concordia, operated under the same ownership as the Triumph, capsized killing 32 people. We were faced with a completely dead ship, a marginally competent captain and a trek of three thousand Americans across a potentially violent Mexican peninsula. Death in a brawl, death by drowning or in the hands of the Mexican cartel, how could Angelica sleep?

Near us, hundreds tossed and turned; they were content we had survived another day, I was not. The fire, explosion and lack of sleep kept me on edge. In the background, the crew concentrated on ship clean up and totting bags of shit away from the cabins. The murmurs of trekking through a dangerous Mexican coast had quieted for the moment as we had the peace of the night. Angelica also slept peacefully while I stared out into the sky unable to release myself from the fear. Out there in the stars I could see the headlights aiming right for me from far away. Only one thing was missing.

11:30 am The Legend

The dubious communiqué.

"Ding, ding, ding."

The thick, choppy and lumbering Tuscan voice of Angelo Los. "Good morning everyone, this is your captain and I wanted to update you on a few items and say that I am really sorry for the accident. We are in radio contact with the tug boat and eh it should be here by noon time and ehh later in the evening we'll have another tugboat arriving from Mobile Alabama, so they both will tow us on the way to Progresso. I will like now to pass you to Jen so she can give you all the random of activities and more information and eh again I am really sorry for the accident. Jen." Captain Los seemed lost and his lack of enthusiasm and optimism was not reassuring.

Jen jumped in with a spark, upbeat and as a determined stiff upper lip Brit. "Thank you very much captain. Well, a very good morning to you ladies and gentlemen I hope you did manage to get some sleep last night despite these challenging conditions. Once again folks a huge thank you for your patience and understanding as you all have been lovely. Just a little bit of updated information not really too much. We have just been on that satellite phone to the Miami head office. First of all, I wanna say a huge big thank you to the technical team, they have been working throughout the night and they have managed to restore some power on board. We have a two elevators now working; we have an elevator on the aft of the ship and mid ship that's working. That's BRILLANT news. There are a few coffee machines working up on the Lido deck which is amazing news! I can now finally get a cup of tea; I have gone so

long without tea. And these guys are continuing to work on this.
Now I know that some of the toilets are working but most of them
are not working. We are trying our very, very, very best to get the
toilet system working. The guys down there are working furiously.
As the captain said the tugboat is scheduled to arrive at 12 noon
today and an additional tugboat will meet up with us later on to
provide extra assistance. This is gonna take us all the way back to
Port Progresso Mexico.   In the meantime our sister ship, the
Legend, will be stopping by to off load some additional supplies.
She is expected to be around the area at about 1 pm today. You
might have noticed as well that the United States Coast Guard cutter
remains in the area and is in contact with us constantly. Also folks
we are in contact we our Miami office for guidance and support and
we got that 24 hotline still available for your people at home. We
are giving them regular updates. The weather conditions today are
phenomenal we couldn't really ask for anything more. It's sunny,
it's warm, it's breezy, it's lovely. You might still notice a slight
listing of the ship. Honestly folks this is nothing to worry about at
all. It's normal. It's just due to the wind and the sea conditions.
There is nothing to worry about there. So, I don't really have any
updated important information for you. We are going to be calling
on that satellite phone every hour and the Miami head office has
promised that as soon as they have any updates on the travel
information from Progresso, I know that's what a lot of you are
waiting on; we will pass that information on to you. For right now
folks the team is working on the Lido deck and were gonna have
some food through out the day. Once again, a huge thank you to all
the very, very, very hard working team members here on board.
They have been going since yesterday morning at 5 o'clock and they

are still going with a smile on their face. So right now get out there and enjoy the morning. We are going to have some activities and trivia games and I'll get back with you soon."

"Ding."

That fear of starving or running out of bottled water briefly abated as we expected to receive help from both the Legend and the Conquest. For a short moment it felt as if we were thrown a life line, but that line quickly become a thin fragile thread as the Legend came into view closing in on the Triumph.

Angelica and I were side by side for over 10 hours, so she went back to her cabin to check on her daughter and I went down to the deck 3 boardwalk to catch a view of the Legend.

The Legend approached quickly from the distance and under full power she was headed straight for us with the bow of the ship pointed squarely at the mid section of the Triumph. As she came in closer and closer the Legend kept its tight course like an arrow set on its target. The Legend was headed straight for us on a collision course.

At less than a mile away the Legend made a quick maneuver in desperation swinging its aft section toward the forward port side of our ship. From deck 3 just beyond eyesight of the Capital Bar I watched the rear of the Legend swing closer and closer toward the hull of the Triumph like a baseball bat in slow motion inches away from a glass window. Passengers crowding the railing of deck 3 gasped and screamed as it **was apparent the Legend would certainly smash into us.**

"I can see into their cabins!" A man near me pointed and hollered.

In its lethargic and urgent emergency turn away from us, the Legend's aft section continued to swing closer and closer to the Triumph's unprotected and vulnerable hull. The Legend would smash into us ripping a gapping hole into the Triumph that would send all of us to the bottom of the ocean killing three thousand aboard the Triumph and another three thousand aboard the Legend.

I was stunned motionless not believing I was a witness to this. I needed to run away from the railing as the Legend's aft section was going to impact where I stood, but my legs could not move. That sinking feeling came over me again knowing that I was going to die alone in this catastrophic ship collision. I knew I could not continue to dodge a deadly fate twice in just as many days. Just as a glimmer of hope was on the horizon the shadow of death quickly shuttered it. My soul was tired and weary from this constant hope of survival and certain chance of death tug-a-war. The Legend grew in my pupils across my sclera until there was nothing to see but the ship as it poked at me in gross magnification. At a thousand feet away, the Legend's engines surged, moaned and croaked fiercely chopping the water between the blades of its propellers as it fought to counter its course into the Triumph. The Legend franticly beat its engines against the ocean spewing crest of water into large white slopes changing the sapphire blue sea into a furious storm of beaten waves as it carried out emergency maneuvers.

Above this terrific site, more people began to scream from the top decks. An emergency alarm echoed across the tight space between the ships.

700 feet away.

"OH MY GOD! THEY'RE GONNA HIT US!" A woman down from me screamed and fainted back on the deck. A shuffle away from the impact sight turned into a panic.

500 feet away.

The scare reached the Legend, as her passengers crowding the aft deck cabins pointed in horror and shock as they were on a direct collision course with the Triumph. They abandoned the aft section of their ship running like rats in a collapsing building. On the top decks of the Legend I could see people in fear run to towards the forward section of the ship. I was close enough to see their shoes, watches and expressions on their faces as they ran.

300 feet away.

I still could not move. Like the first the night of darkness I wasn't afraid of dying quickly and tragically. I feared dying alone, slowly and in closed quarters, and again the realization that I could do nothing suffocated me. That car was barreling down the deck for me, but this time it was not going to stop – it was going to run me over at full speed!

The massive Legend, nearly 963 feet in length, weighing over 88,000 tons also carrying over 3,000 souls was less than 250 feet away at full power and swinging toward our helpless bobbing ship. A collision at sea would be catastrophic.

The Legend's rear propeller furiously swung into the water as the ship's rear end sloshed through the waves fighting to miss the Triumph. It beat the life out of the sea trying to miss our ship.

At 230 feet away we were sitting ducks and helpless. I imagined the crash in my brain ripping the ship in two and sinking us into a whirl pool in the middle of the ocean.

I held my breath for several seconds, closed my eyes as if to pray and opened them again as the Legend closed in. It was too close to call; the Legend would hit us or barely miss us.

At 150 feet the Legend barely missed the Triumph. 150 feet in the open sea!

If I had a breath I would exhale, I had none so I gnashed my teeth in anger.

A man next me pushed me in the back grabbing my shoulder as he wiped his sweated brow. "Shit that was close!" He said exhaling for both of us forcing a small wisp of air up from my chest. "No way was that planned! Are they trying to kill us?!"

I was frustrated and stressed and the stress shifted my depression into overdrive. All these people would have died. That sinking feeling that would not go away came from having our lives completely in the hands of these idiots. The Devil's Ride was coming with a fury and this time I held out my arms for it to take me!

Deck 3 grumbled with the anger and dissatisfaction of passengers who were at their wits end. Imprisoned passengers walked about in the white robes of the state, sleeping where they could, when they could, upset at the lies we were being told and the Captain's mismanagement of the situation. Sleep derived, I hadn't rested or bathed in three days. We were at their mercy. It was Guantanamo on the Sea. We were little more than detainees subject to the torture of Carnival's 'Enhanced Sailing Techniques'!

Hot, angry and smelling like a sewer, I ran the course of the ship pushing through passengers to get to my cabin.   It was uninhabitable but the only place I could hide, find a modicum of privacy and scream.

With my door propped open, in the dim light from the hallway, I opened my last bottle of champagne and waited to drown my consciousness inside of it hoping for some form of release and to be able to breathe, but before I could there was something else I had to deal with.

Down the stretch everyone hung out a foot, a hand or head into the hallway like restless prisoners. My neighbors argued in their cabin and banged against the walls saying. "This feels like prison!"

I peeked my head out to a dark and dank chasm gloomily lit by emergency exit signs that highlighted human figures that would reach into the darkness and suddenly jump back into a dark hole. I knew where I was and what was haunting me for the past couple of days and something that I realized at that moment drove a major part of my depression. The Triumph, it was in fact a prison and I knew prisons very well. The main effects of prisons are that you are alone, in whatever may happen to you. Bad relationships are a prison. Bad jobs are a prison. Depression is a prison, but this prison was very specific and very specific to me. The feeling of drowning in water, the old woman and her family from New Orleans the day before, passengers dressed in white robes or wrapped in white sheets and long desolate hallways speckled with open doors protruding limbs of the restless crowded my sanity.

In the face of a tragedy a matter of minutes can reveal a lifetime and in that moment it was 2005.

Hurricane Katrina and Rita

In 2005, I was caught and in jail in Beaumont. As Hurricane Katrina, a category 5 major storm, raged against New Orleans, hundreds of thousands of people fled Louisiana into Texas past Beaumont and into Houston. Hundreds of people died in the water as the levies broke and a city unprepared for the rising water waited in the balance. In just under a month another category 5 hurricane, Rita, churned in the Atlantic and made its course for the Gulf Coast. As if to wipe those who fled New Orleans off the map permanently, Rita aimed for the route between Houston, Beaumont and Lake Charles.

As Hurricane Rita arrived, the city of Beaumont went under a mandatory evacuation. With just hours away from landfall I watched a city of millions flee on crowded highways. As far away as Houston the freeways were solid walls of cars and trucks headed away from the coast. It was a wrenching and soul killing feeling for me to see everyone I knew and loved move away as I stood there waiting for disaster to come, alone, and knowing none of them were thinking about me. As with those left behind in New Orleans there was no plan for us in Beaumont. We were the most vulnerable because our location was a temporary jail facility made mostly of tin and cinder block and could by not withstand a category 5 hurricane.

Hurricane Rita was expected to hit Beaumont with its full force by 3:15 p.m. At 1:30 p.m. the city was empty and the sky completely dark. A brisk rain and strong winds pounded our facility that now had a minimal staff with no food, no power, no plumbing, no water pressure and no plan. The Triumph. At 2:45 the staff had come up with a course of action. A brick and mortar prison, a fortress by all definitions, was less than three miles away across a thin prairie. As the outer rings of Rita pummeled Beaumont, the small guard staff handcuffed 375 of us together in a long line and pushed us across the field, through the hurricane. It was a loud, deafening, thunderous and uproarious experience. Sand bags that were laid by our destination unit a day before lifted and danced in the wind knocking us over. As the winds picked up, the bags shattered open in grenade styled explosions against the prison walls. By the time we arrived at the prison, power was out, there was no food or water, the toilets did not flush and puddles on the floor formed lakes, and the waters of the lakes were on the rise. The Triumph's long dark hallways were reminiscent of the prison hallways that led into the low laying day room were I listened to Beaumont get plowed by Rita as the hurricane's water rose up, over my feet, past my ankles, approaching my knees and past my knees. Around me everyone was dressed in white by either wrapping themselves in sheets or the wardrobe of the state. The fear and possibility of drowning at the bottom of that prison was real. We knew we could drown. In a moment of compassion at 6:30 p.m. the staff released us from the cuffs. Fearful of their own lives they joined us and waited. The storm passed and 36 hours later we emerged, exhausted, hungry and with a dirt water line up to our waist. The city took a big hit and our facility across the way was twisted and destroyed.

"This feels like prison!" I heard my neighbor down the hall again.

Sitting in my doorway I dripped the champagne onto a gag. I tied it tight and sipped the cheap drink in small gulps while listening to Mahler.

Throwing my head back I took a deep swig from the bottle. After a second gulp I peeled the orifice from my lips and poured its contents across my face hoping to kill the stench of crap, urine and burned fuel and metal that saturated deck 8. It didn't work. A trickle of passengers ran by me and headed to the aft section of the ship and outside to deck 9. I followed them to a mass of people pushed against the railings with their phones pressed against their face. The Legend was also outfitted with a satellite transmitter system and while she was in range we were able to pass our signals through. Some got through, most did not.

I had no one to call but seeing the express agony of people around me pushed me into a deep internal silence. I was still on the ride.

I went down to the bar on deck 5 and was greeted by Dutch and The Aggie Lawyer and chatted with them as I waited for Angelica.

The Sista's from Houston sat on the bar trying to get a signal. One of the girls held up her phone towards the rear window and I could see STEPDAD written across the screen. She pulled it down in a frustration. "Have you been able to reach anyone?" She asked me.

I nodded but secretly knew that when the call log got down to *stepdad*, it was bad. "I think it depends on your carrier. Some people have gotten through, but most have not." I told her.

She tapped her phone changing some settings and tried again. "Nothing! They say we will be back at Port Progresso by tomorrow evening, which is good because I don't think I can take another day on this ship. If all goes well we could be home by Wednesday evening." The other one said.

The younger sister made a face and didn't even try her phone. They were close. They kept looking at each other as to confirm they were still there and that they were still alive and with each other.

"You two are here alone?" I asked the older.

Her younger sister looked at her as she answered. "Yes. My mom and stepdad couldn't come so it's just us."

"How do you like it?" I asked.

"Hate it!" Both of them answered in unison.

"Where's your girlfriend? She was in here looking for you." The older asked.

I started my response but was cut off. "That's not my girl.."

"We see the way you two look at each other. When you are together it's almost as if you don't even see what's going on around here." The older sister said.

"Yea, it's romantic." The younger teased. "Too bad you can't find any personal time around here."

"It already smells like ass everywhere!" The older one shot in response leaning over and slapping hands with her sister.

The crowd laughed as she brought us some cheer.

From the rear window of the ship just under its name I watched the Legend and the Conquest circle around us in the distance. Angry, agitated and hungry, my nerves were frayed and I could now see this same feeling on the people around me. I left and took the path through the Big Easy Piano Bar but paused briefly to take in the large Muhammad Ali painting hanging on the hall passageway. It took me back to Friday's art auction and the "Norton Chasing Ali in Yankee Stadium" print I wanted. That day now felt like a lifetime away. I could hardly remember the elegant voyage as it started, now only this horror remained. Yet, from this horror an angel appeared.

"I heard there was some excitement out there?" Angelica caught me in the hallway.

I wanted to scream. What's worst than depression is trying to control your fear. One half of your life force has failed you and you are forced to acknowledge it, while the other half fights to control it. I fought not to just scream and in a subdued voice said. "It was a close call. Really touchy there." I wanted to scream.

Angelica smiled and lit my soul. "Oh. Mr. Calm and Cool, nothing gets to you does it? Well, that's good." She came in close. "Is that a new cologne? I had to take some time to freshen up also, but yours smell better."

Angelica always took me away from a brief moment. She had changed clothes slipping into a nice pair of tight fitting jeans and white long sleeve shirt. She was beautiful and graceful. We went top side and waited in line three hours for a cold veggie sandwich.

The Sista's were right, when Angelica was around everything else disappeared. We danced around each other like Mahler's point and counter point. In this life and in this place we were perfect for each other, but this wasn't reality it was some dark shitty bucket disconnected from the world and leant half over bobbing in the ocean.

This was the ride, this is how depression works. There is always a moment of hope that makes me want to seize the moment and take control of the situation instead of just enjoying the moment when it comes. It is the lure of the life line that starts it. I take the bait and get in the car thinking I can handle it and I never can. Then comes the anger and I was angry now and even as Angelica softly lifted me away with her voice my mind and my body was still down there on deck 3 waiting for the Legend to smash into us. Depression takes you down brick by brick, loosing the cement of resistance. Some bricks are torn away, some just fall aside. Being in a bad situation was never enough to unravel me; it was always the accompanying message that loosened the mortar.

"You're not eating." Angelica brought me back to her. "I haven't seen you eat all day. I am starving, but I can't swallow another one of these cold things. Everyone is looking for those working toilets. My daughter and I walked around the whole ship and found one, but using it is another matter. The smell is so strong in there we couldn't take it. We did however get a couple bottles of water."

I loved Angelica's optimism. She didn't necessarily see the glass as half full; she saw water in the glass and she was thirsty. She gave me a small bottle of water and three cookies. "Oh wow! I have been looking for some cookies." I felt better, until.

"Ding, ding, ding."

It was Jen. "Good afternoon everyone. We have a few important updates and could I have everyone's attention.   As you might have noticed the tugboats did not arrive on schedule. Apparently, we have drifted farther off course than we originally anticipated and we have some updates on that also. We have been in contact with our home office and it seems the plan has changed a little. The tugboats are expected to arrive by late this evening and by that time we would have drifted further away from Port Progresso in the direction towards Cuba. We could make the trip back to Port Progresso arriving late tomorrow Tuesday night. The other option is to take another day and be towed to port at Mobile Alabama. The home office has made the decision to bring us to port in Mobile, Alabama. They think that it is a better option for everyone. So we will have an extra day at most at sea and I promise we will make that as comfortable as possible for everyone. Updates on our arrival into Mobile, Alabama and further accommodations will be given once the tugboat arrives from Mexico. In the meantime, The Legend has finished off loading supplies to us and she will be giving us a big send off in just a few minutes. We would like everyone on deck to give them a send off also."

"Ding."

"Great another day." I let out in exasperation. "They're not telling us anything. Let me guess the tugboats are just late enough to make the decision real easy about what to do with us." I said.

"Didn't you say you needed more time? Well, now you have it." Her voice was cracking under the pressure. "You will get a chance to finish that novel you are working on and get some rest. Not to mention all the Earl Grey and cookies you can stand. You just seem so well adjusted, almost comfortable. Honestly, I don't see how you do it. I mean I'm falling apart and Zee isn't much better. I am worried sick about my son and.."

"And your husband." I said cutting her off. "You still love him don't you? I mean after all that time how could you not?" I asked her.

"Pat, see how you are now. I wish I could be like you and have the strength to control it and to move on, but I just can't, especially now. I wish I could have your strength and not let these things drive me like this. I can't escape it or deal with it." She said.

I could see it and feel it. Headlights were shining on the glass at the entrance to Club Rio, but this time they were aiming for Angelica. I had to do something.

"I wish I could have your patience and your love Angelica. In the meantime I can give you this." I said and I gave her one cookie back.

Tears welled in her eyes. "How did you know I wanted one? I could only get these three and when I got them I wanted to give them all to you because of how much you looked for sweets and you only wanted this, but I wanted to eat one so bad, but I didn't and now you give me one. Even before you've eaten one you offered one to me."

"I would give them all to you also. I'm not as hungry as I was before and what's the use of having a cookie if you can't share it. Besides, I enjoy your company." I told her.

"You don't have to do this to keep me here. I'm not going anywhere." She told me.

"You were right. I was scared and afraid. I get afraid that I'd never see you again and that loneliness hurts. That fear is a gapping hole inside of me and when you are around there is not as much pain. With you I feel like a part of something and not like a piece of something. I want to go everywhere with you and be everywhere with you but most of all I want to be right here with you." I said.

Angelica smiled and ate her cookie, I ate mine and we split the last one.

After a while the bar emptied, swelled some and emptied again but never reaching anymore than a couple dozen people. Angelica and I were talking again, playing cards and dominoes in between long verbal excursions into our future lives and ambitions. The bar's rear window became our movie screen and from that window we were flying again far into the distance, far away from the Triumph. We went to all the places we wanted to see in our life and we went there by sea, via the Triumph. We visited the mountain ranges near the coast of Peru, around Argentina, to Brazil across the Atlantic to the

Ivory Coast of Africa, to Spain, Paris France, Italy, Rome, Greece, Egypt and back down to Madagascar.

Mahler and The Dabhol

"Your music is still playing." Angelica said pulling at the cord. "What is it? It sounds romantic."

"No, it's not romantic." I smiled back gently.

"You like classical? It's intense and so full of life. It sounds passionate and romantic to me."

"Mahler?" I perked in surprise. "It's his symphony number 1. Passionate, yes, but I wouldn't describe it as romantic. It has been playing for days and I'm trying to get all the way through it but I keep getting interrupted."

Angelica came in closer to me and tilted her head on my shoulder listening.

We joined in the middle of the third movement and as Mahler went on, a small boat squeezed into the rear window moving from the port side and positioning itself a few hundred feet behind the Triumph.

It was the Dabhol, a 107 foot khaki topped tugboat from Port Progresso Mexico. A large Mexican climbed down from The Dabhol's bridge and began waving his straw hat wildly from side to side signaling the driver to position the craft in line with the Triumph. After a few minutes they made the connection and the Dabhol's engine revved to its highest beat tightening the rope between us and them.

Angelica and I listened to the third movement going into the fourth as a small crowd gathered around the bar to watch the spectacle.

The line tightened and in a fury The Dabhol pulled, jerked and yanked at the Triumph.

The fourth movement started and Angelica sat up placing her hand over her heart. "My goodness Mahler!"

The Mexican jumped up and down beating his hat against the wind wildly in an excitement as if the ship was about to explode! The Dabhol strained and yanked under full power tossing up a storm of waves. The tiny ship waxed and waned in the water swinging widely from side to side under the duress of the tight rope.

"PULL DABHOL PULL!" The crowd chanted.

"PULL DABHOL PULL!" More people joined in pumping their fist.

"PULL DABHOL PULL!"

The Dabhol fought against the tide, the Dabhol fought against the rope, the Dabhol fought against the Triumph. The little tug was as tough as a mastiff latched to the tail of an elephant as it tried to forcibly drag it away. We were but tics landed upon the dead beast watching the dog fight this tug of war.

"PULL DABHOL PULL!" The crowd continued.

After a few pulls the ropes tension reached deck five and we could feel the ship gently pulsing with the vibration of the Dabhol's strain.

"PULL DABHOL PULL!" Applause and celebration erupted around the window.

We were moving. It was just a little movement, barely detectable, but it was movement. The dog was dragging the elephant.

The Dabhol steadied us away from the sun falling in the horizon and as night came the thick darkness of the sky covered the ship. Night time was difficult. The darkness seemed to get inside me as it wrapped my around us like a murky cloak.

Angelica and I went out to deck 10 and took our position like the night before, and watched the Dabhol pull us through the stars.

Tuesday, February 12, 2013

Alcohol & Depression

The brawl in the bar

In the early morning hours, another tugboat, the Pioneer Resolve joined the Dabhol. Jen informed us we were now moving at a snail's pace of about six knots per hour and we should arrive in Mobile, Alabama mid day Thursday. No one cared to listen to the announcements as frustrations grew to its highest levels. If we had gone to Port Progresso we would be on dry land by now, if only at the port. Food supplies from the Legend was gone, there was still no fresh water, no power and no toilets. Dirt, grim, shit and piss permeated every inch of the ship, everything and everyone. The Triumph's inside was a thick fog of choking puke so pungent it caused instant nausea.

I was sick. I couldn't breathe and a nagging cough jumped out from me unexpectedly every few minutes. Making my life worst, I hadn't slept in days nor bathed so a thin film settled on my skin. A thick mucus rolled from my face so I went to the infirmary on deck 1. The line outside of the infirmary was long and packed with those like me who could not breathe and choked on every exhale. There were also a lot of bumps and bruises from slips caused by pissy stairwells and slick walkways. After a short screening; I saw the nurse and a doctor who gave me a blister pack of the classic red Sudafed tablets and some acetaminophen. Before I could reach the stairs I popped two of the Sudafed and begged for a sudden explosion in my sinuses so I could breathe. It never came.

All day everyone continued to search for food, but there was none. The bottled water was gone and I couldn't drink another hot soda. Shops in the mall on deck 5 opened briefly, taking cash only and evaporated their supplies of candy, medicine and chips within minutes.

The crew, working every shift, had to abandon their cabins in the lower decks and now all slept on the tables and chairs in the London and Paris dining halls. After three days they were just as tired as we were but still managed to keep busy cleaning the ship wiping down door knobs and handles with three day old buckets of bleach and water. A never ending trail of red bio-hazard bags full of shit followed behind those buckets and the people who carried them, but their enthusiasm was beginning to wane also. ALL of the staff was forced into the rotation of cleaning and dolling out cold veggie sandwiches. The stage performers manned the buffet and smiled generously and happily at seeing passengers come through and compliment them on their show. Jimmie and Jessica scowled at their new assignments slicing bread and plying thick layers on mustard and ketchup.

Back at the bar a few more people found our charging outpost. Young Orson Welles, a student from the University of Houston, donning a fedora sat at the bar puffing at a vapor cigar and enchanted everyone with stories of how this experience would play in the theatres.

"It's a comedy, no a tragedy, no a comic tragedy." He wailed drawing a few laughs. "Really, I don't know if we are faring any better or any worst at this point. We go to Mexico and they want to bus us through cartel infested territory to get home. A ship comes to save us and almost hits us, we have no power but they are in communications with the home office every minute. Two days ago three small cans of soda costs minimum wage and now we are bathing with the sodas. We have nothing to eat or drink while fucking English Jen sips tea on the bridge. I'm sorry '*a proper spot of tea*'. Has anyone seen her? Really? Has anyone seen her? I have and she looks exactly like she sounds. A short red head British **..brilliant** but inferior ninny that I'd like to say PISS OFF too. I can go on."

The Aggie Lawyer joined in with some optimism. "We do have two tugs now."

"Yea, but where are we going?" The younger Sista voiced.

Angelica grabbed my arm, pulled close to me and said. "It does seem like things are getting better."

I noticed a man, Morn, sitting alone, quiet and still at the far end of the bar. He was always there everyday looking out the back window in a comatose sadness never speaking nor looking at anyone. He sat at the bar in a misery gone to another life.

My depression made me sensitive to other people's depression, especially those who were suffering at maniac levels. To me, they were my silent friends, quiet companions that walked next to me like shadows. Though we never talk I always know they are there. They confirm I am among them and at the same time kept my ass in line. I felt the waves of this man's depression blow through me. He was on the outside what I was on the inside, unhappy, in turmoil and suffering. He was on the edge and could go either way. My depression did not let me enjoy the moment but Angelica and the markedly good-humor of the crowd gave me a moment of pause, but just a moment.

"Ding, ding, ding."

It was Jen. "Good evening everyone, I have some updates and fantastic news for everyone. We have been in contact with our home office and they have given us some fantastic news so please listen closely. For all of our passengers 21 and older we have decided to open the bars and offer free drinks. Fantastic! So beginning, in um just about 10 minutes you may visit the Capital bar on deck 3 or the two bars on deck 5 and drink it up! And as you know, we still have no electricity so all drinks for the evening are on the house! So, when you have time why don't you pop in to one of the bars and have a drink, relax and enjoy."

"Ding."

In the silence after the last ding everyone looked around to each other and realized we were in the bar, the largest bar on the ship and so far not too many people had come through.

A crowd began to form across the room at the glass doors across from the lounge area.

"Take it down! Take it down!" Dutch yelled across to me to dismantle the power strips before the crowd rushed us.

I complied and jumped behind the bar.

Within seconds, we swelled from 32 at the bar to over 300 in the lounge and more coming. Two crew members came behind the bar and opened the liquor lockers and lined single serve glasses along the bar. When I looked up Angelica was squeezed out by the crowd. The air in the room became tight. The two crew members poured and poured and poured and poured. They threw back empty bottles of tequila, vodka, whiskey, and liquors so fast the trash cans and sinks were quickly filled.

The glasses emptied faster then they could be filled as the crowd became rowdy! 400 hundred people pressed against the bar as a melee erupted with passengers pushing, shoving and fighting for a next in line spot.

Young Orson Welles grabbed the handles on the bar to keep his position as a gang of hands grabbed him. I looked through the crowd for Angelica and screamed her name and when I came back to Young Orson Welles and he was gone – snatched!

The two crew members could not pour fast enough so they began sliding the bottles across the bar further inciting the crowd to fight and they did.

Smacks, pops, slaps and gut punches ripped through the crowd coming from men and women of all sizes as the two crew members tried to keep up with demand.

"Are you just going to sit back there? Pass the shit!" A man yelled at me.

This had me thinking. *"How fast could I get up to my cabin and grab my duffle bag?"* The outer hull stairwell was just a couple feet away so I slipped out of the side door dashed up to deck 8 and came back down in less than two minutes. By that time, several fights had broken out across the lounge but the pile up at the lines prevented them from climbing over the bar, so I slipped back in and stuffed my bag with bottles.

A woman screamed in the lounge. A man yelled that that was his wife. Another man shouted back he didn't give a fuck. The bar, the lounge, the rear outer stairwells and the lobby filled with the angry depressed looking for a drink. The scene was rot and ugly, turning Lord of The Flies to Lord of The Rings. The women argued, the men pushed and fought and they all scrambled on each other in an uproar like their life was on the line. They were so pressed on each other it was hard to raise an arm, much less a fist, or else the melee would have been much worst.

Security finally arrived, rather a contingent of concierge with safety vest and flash lights. The leader among them, part of the security staff, was a very tall uniformed female officer that barked orders in a deep Ukrainian accent. She pushed through the crowd moving most of the men away in a single thrust. The crowd urged the two crew members to move faster with the bottles.

"Close the bar! Close the bar!" The security officer yelled wading through the crowd but two crewmen could not hear her.

Several men held a line against the woman preventing her from getting closer to the bar. She pushed against them, they locked arms and the whole section waved to the side.

The security officer eventually broke through. "Close the fucking bar!" She slammed her hand down on the wood snapping the two crewmen to attention.

The last few bottles on the bar were grabbed up as the security team moved the crowd away from the bar and into the lounge and adjacent corridors. I zipped my duffle bag and again moved toward the outer stairwell, but just before I left I looked across the scene in horror as the crowd dispersed. Seeing the anguish on their faces stirred my depression, but this time I didn't feel happy as they were at my level, I felt pity and sorry at the human condition. Morn was still at the bar sitting alone in the corner. He cradled a bottle of whiskey in his arms and had a smile as big as the port side of the ship.

The smell in my cabin had gotten sharper over the last day. It was pungent and piercing like a decomposing body. The mood on deck 8 was just as thick. My neighbors with the kids were fighting again. The little ones Molly and Chad continued to run the dark hallway splashing piss along the way. Their parents could not contain their frustration and anger with the situation. She was upset he wasn't doing enough and he didn't want to be there. The two of them pushed around in the dark room stomping on the floor and beating their fists on anything they came across.

"I'm leaving and I'm taking the boys with me!" The man yelled.

The woman stepped a foot into the hallway and took to the P.A. system. "Molly!! Molly!! Come back down here so you can see your father abandon us on this damn ship!"

"I am not abandoning you!" He shouted to her from inside the room.

The woman pounded the five steps from the hallway to the cabin bathroom and locked herself inside. "I should have never gotten on this ship! This was your idea and now you want to just drop us and walk off! I can't believe this is happening!"

I could not believe the woman locked herself in the bathroom. My bathroom was two inches thick with piss and shit for three days, just opening the door was a death sentence.

She stayed in the lavatory whining, crying and blubbering. My face contorted and collapsed just thinking about the conditions in a four by five locked box with no air or water and human waste sitting for days. The man gathered a bag and took the two of the boys with him. Molly stayed behind beating on the bathroom door for her mother.

The couple across the hall from me picked up on the action from my neighbor and began to raise their voices.

"You should do something!" The woman yelled.

"There is nothing I can do!" He shot back.

"You're useless!" She stabbed.

The man stormed out, slammed the cabin door and headed up to deck 9.

After the man left, the corridor was quiet for a few minutes until arguments began to carry throughout the hallway. Now everyone was arguing.

Jen made an announcement stating the bars were closed and urged us to pull together and share food, water, diapers and baby formula but I could barely hear her over the shouting so I went up to deck 9 with a small bottle of bourbon. The two men from my section sat by the pool drinking sodas and ranting.

"Be glad you are here by yourself." My neighbor said to me. "And I'm sorry for the noise and for the kids. This was supposed to be our coming back together vacation but it's turning into a break up nightmare. She just can't keep her cool and it sets me off."

"Meet my brother-in-law." The other one joked. "I wish I had time to get down there and get a drink before they closed the bar."

"I have this." I brandished the bottle.

My neighbor lost track of his kids and followed the bottle as it waved in my hand. His *brother-in-law* saw a glass oasis filled with caramel colored liquid nutrients. I left them the bottle. They broke the seal, mixed the drinks and smiled.

Angelica came back to our spot on deck 10 and reminded me she didn't drink but wished she did because the pulls from the Dabhol were making her sea sick and dizzy. Her red eyes waved a little every time a vibration came up from the floor. "How do you feel?" She asked me.

"I still have not slept but I think the medicine is helping some. One minute I can barely stand from exhaustion and in the next I cannot close my eyes, but I do feel better when I see you. I got worried when the crowd took over down there. I didn't want to see you get hurt. I don't ever want to see you hurt." I told her.

Angelica tried to smile, but said. "I went back to my cabin and stayed there to try to get myself together. I don't want to cry anymore. I am almost all cried out. It's this. This, all of this, there is no food, no water, the air is bad and the fights are getting worst. People are yelling and screaming and everyone is on edge. I just can't take it. I miss my baby boy and my family. I don't know what's going to happen. I can feel them hurting for me and I am hurting for them. When I see how these people are acting it makes me feel like I am back in our relationship when it was really bad. Before we were married my husband and I broke up and I stayed with a friend for awhile. It was nothing serious between me and the other guy but my husband found out and he came for me. He came for me and was angrier than I have ever seen him. I was trapped. These people are just like that, all of them. They don't know how to love and let go. Love of all things is not selfish. It is selfless. Love is something you give, not something you take away. When you get the message that forces you to want to take it, you want it all for yourself, you want to control it, but the more you try to control it, the less control you have of it. It's not too unlike depression, you have to see it and recognize what it is. You have to let it go and let love flourish inside of you first. If it's not inside of you first you will always be afraid, and you can't be afraid and in love. A selfless act of love cures all."

In one minute she was sad and in the next beautiful. I heard the words she was saying but all I wanted was to hold her and kiss your face and her lips while she talked. The more she spoke of pushing love away I thought of grabbing hold of it. I made my move and pulled her close to me, but Angelica kept talking about releasing her burdens and the way life should be. Close to her head I again could smell the enchanting fragrance of her hair. I took several deep breathes to take in more and each was intoxicating as the last one. An hour passed and I hadn't recognized she had been asleep for the last fifty minutes. Across the deck, the white sheets of the floating shantytown gently flapped and popped in the wind while our floating lantern, the Dabhol chugged along.

Wednesday, February 13, 2013

Movie night- fight night

I had not slept since Friday night and by midday Wednesday exhaustion showed heavily upon me. My eyes were consistently red, moved slowly and sagged under duress. A strain in the back of my neck bulged to a hill as an unyielding numbness coursed from my toes to my scalp. The residue of the ships putrid environment stuck to my skin greasing it with a toxic grime that adhered to everything I touched.

On the inside I was back where I was a week earlier. I was in the car, The Devil's Ride; seat belted in the front watching the wheels and fender pummel my life off the road while I was helpless to intervene. There was nothing to do on the ship but wait; I waited for food, I waited for water, I waited for a breath of fresh air and I waited for hope.

The crew was directed to remove the shantytown topping the Triumph. The homemade tents of white sheets covering the Triumph from stern to keel were ordered removed so a United States Coast Guard helicopter could safely approach. The Coast Guard Cutter Vigorous joined us and would escort us the remaining way to Mobile Alabama, as the helicopter evacuated a passenger and dropped supplies.

The Triumph looked bare almost naked in comparison to the days before.

More details of our reparations and disembarkation were released; however, I was not convinced of any it. Too many lies, an abundance of misdirection and misinformation had comprised Jen's integrity. We were still too far away to reach out to the hope of being home again which according to Jen was still more than 36 hours away, an eternity.

Because of the open bar fiasco the night before more people knew about our trickling power supply. Jen took full advantage of this and decided to bring the *fun* to our spot by arranging a few short stage shows and boot leg movies projected from a crewmembers laptop. The lounge modestly filled as we voted on which movies to watch. A couple of kids movies would come beginning with Toy Story 3, then as the evening turned into night, more adult suitable titles would play. Hoping to lift our spirits, Angelica and I sat together in anticipation of the movies and shows.

"A few movies would be great. I need a connection to the outside world and this one is one of my favorites." Angelica leaned over and whispered with a wink. "One of the main characters name is the same as mine and Johnny Depp is sooo cute."

I looked around, The Sista's had come in and taken a booth. Elle came in also and I hadn't seen her in days. I watched everyone and everything except the movie and Angelica took notice of this.

"Cheer up Pat." She said in a comforting tone trying to pull me in. "It's our first movie date. You should learn how to relax, enjoy the moment and have a laugh."

I hadn't seen any of the movies scheduled to play and this was not my idea of making a connection to the outside world but I enjoyed seeing Angelica smile. The movie wasn't enough to raise me out of my lingering depression because when other people were happy around me I couldn't join in with them. Everyone seemed happier at least on the surface. I was not happy. After a few minutes I had the urge to see the sun set for what I hoped would be the last time from this ship. I wrote Angelica a note to meet me at our spot on deck 10 after the first movie. I took the long walk around deck 5 again. The Triumph was a dark waste land, a useless rotting and choking hull that smoked of an anal sphincter, one suddenly tied at both ends with all of us caught in between.

Along the rail alone I watched the sun dip in the distance with no land in site as the Triumph gently and slowly pulsed along. I looked forward to the hot meal, hot bath and a good night's sleep in Mobile Alabama and being home by Thursday night. Thinking about it made my old life start to come back to me. It was right there just a few yards off to the right of the Dabhol. I could see myself back at work in the warehouse fighting to make ends meet. I could see the long sleepless nights alone. Sleep. I was so tired I couldn't feel the difference between the stress that that life once brought and the hell I was in. I could barely stand and blinking my eyes was problematical.

Angelica didn't show to the rail and after awhile I felt she hadn't realized I left her the note. When I returned to the lounge Dark Shadows was ending. Angelica watched my every step as I moved through the crowd from the lounge doors to the stools at the door.

"I can't do it." She whispered over to me keeping her eyes on the stage. "I can't do it. I feel like if I had gone out there with you, this time, I might never come back. In all this time you have never asked me for anything. You are always here when I need you. You listen to my problems and my life. You listen and you don't judge nor tell me what to do. I could love you for that alone. You are not forcing yourself on me. You are kind and gentle. For some reason I just trust you and I don't know why. Yet, there it is, I see it behind your eyes, the depression you are dealing with. You are afraid of something. I think that you are afraid of holding on and not being able to let go. You think if you grab on you'll never let go." She said.

"I always grab on. That is what you are supposed to do. If you care about someone you should let them know. They should never have a doubt that you care about them. That's how I am. I will always be here for you." I told her.

"I know you care about me. I haven't let go of my husband and no matter what he has done I don't want to be like him. I need out of this hell first because I don't want to take you through it. I know you think you can save me, but I need to save myself first. You don't hurt the people you love." She told me.

"And you don't want to hurt him?" I asked her.

"No Pat, I don't want to hurt you. I can see our life together, being happy in either Texas or Arizona as long as we are together. I see it and I want it so bad but I have to force myself to see what would happen before we could get to that. You have been so lucky to see the things that have been controlling your life and I have been so lucky to see the things I am missing in my life. The trip would destroy us before we arrived at our destination. And I don't want that to happen. Till then, we have this trip, one that has brought us together and has taken us to so many places. Be strong with me because we still have more places to go, like our first movie date." She said.

Angelica was able to passionately articulate the deep feelings we both shared; she was able to kindle the fire without turning it ablaze. My depression had a tight grip on me, but she showed me how to pay attention to my triggers and how to not be afraid of seeing them. I was still in the car taking the ride, but for the first time ever on this long endless street I had come to a stop sign and Angelica ran over and beat on the window and yelled GET OUT! GET OUT! In response to her, I asked. "What movie will we see?"

"Grown Ups. Have you seen it before?" She asked.

"No I haven't." I said.

Angelica grabbed my hand, pulled me close to her and said. "It's a classic, very funny and you'll love it."

I brandished a smile in the beginning but later joined her in some big laughs as we tapped and nudged each other through the night.

I popped open the door and set one foot out of the car.

After Grown Ups, Jen arrived and blessed the efforts of the staff and crew in their hard work over the past few days. She went on for several minutes to make sure we all were completely convinced we were in no danger and everything was being handled

FANTASTICALLY. It was the first time I heard her voice without being nervous that she was hiding the truth from us and that disaster loomed just around the corner. There was something about her voice that immediately invited an eerie chaos.

It was late and most of the lounge was still awake and a couple dozen or so people including Angelica and I stayed at the bar. We all wanted the movies to keep playing so the crew member with the laptop selected Taken 2. The movie started and before Jen could get too far away a riot erupted in the lounge.

"This is my home and I want to get some sleep!" A woman jumped up from the floor throwing her sheets into the air. "It is time for everyone to leave RIGHT NOW! If I have to sleep in here on the floor every night all of you will have to get out of here. Movie night is OVER! I don't have a cabin to go to so everybody out!"

"Bitch shut up!" Someone yelled. "We want to see the show!"

"You wanna see a show? You wanna see a show! I'll give you a show!" The woman ran to the stage in front of the projection and started singing the Canadian national anthem at the top of her voice.

"Get off the fucking stage!" A voice cried.

"O Canada – O Canada, we stand on guard for thee!" She kept going stomping on the stage and knocking the laptop over.

"Move your ass!" The lounge became rowdy. "Somebody get security!"

Everyone hurled insults at her further inflaming the woman to dance and sing more of the anthem.

The concierge finally arrived with flashlights and tried to talk the woman down, but she wouldn't relent. "I want these people out of here!" She yelled. "O Canada – O Canada! We stand on guard for thee!"

The Ukrainian security officer arrived and without any discussion snatched the woman down. "You want to sleep! I will lock you up where you can get a good night's sleep!" She tossed the woman by the arm.

"You can't do this to me! I'm not leaving! O Canada! O Canada!" The demented woman continued.

"Take her away! Take her away! Take her away!" The crowd chanted.

The Ukrainian obliged pulling her off into the lobby.

"Ding."

Thursday, February 14, 2013

The Final Push. Stronger.

1 pm

Angelica and I spent the night and morning together and because of Taken 2 and our Ukrainian friend, we toured the other half of the world. We put our arms around each other and sailed through the sky in folded paper plane with the word Triumph scribbled on the side. In 5 days she never left my side and I never left her.

Anxiety reached its highest point by midday Thursday. Angelica's heart raced in anticipation of finally being close to land and having a conclusion to this fiasco aboard the Triumph. I just wanted to breathe, be clean and be somewhere where I could let my guard down and get some peace of mind and sleep. The expectation that that would finally occur continued to build, but I was not home yet. In the distance, the United States Coast Guard Cutter Vigorous circled and once we reached US waters armed members of the Coast Guard came aboard with members of the US Department of Customs. They were there to insure order and cooperation on the ship and to assist with the disembarkation process. We met them with cheers and applause.

As we pulled closer to Mobile Alabama the air outside of the ship became just as thick and dirty as the air on the inside and nothing could disguise that, or the deep blue of the ocean turning into the tan silt of the Gulf Coast.

4pm

Angelica and I stayed together through the customs process that took place outside of the lounge on deck 5. Since she was on a lower deck than me she would disembark before me so we spent as much time as we could together. We held hands and talked until the ship came within cellular range. Within seconds her phone started to buzz with missed calls and text messages. Tears formed in Angelica's eyes as she tried to reach her family and after talking to her baby boy she wavered and swooned so I got her a chair.

Sitting there, I massaged her shoulder with one hand as she held my other hand close to her heart and talked on the phone. She cried and squeezed the color from my fingers as she talked to different family members and friends until finally her phone died. "I need to get some rest." She said.

"I do too. I can't seem to shake this headache and taking these meds on an empty stomach is making me sick. While you were on the phone Jen informed us we will not be able to get off the ship until after midnight. It appears we still have plenty of time. They lied to us again and this is really aggravating me. We also will not be staying in Mobile Alabama, nor will we go home from here. They are going to immediately put us on buses to New Orleans, another three hours away and sort everything out from there. " I said. "Unless you have someone here to receive you."

"No I don't. All of this is so crazy." Angelica took a moment to breathe and continued saying. "You know Pat, two days ago it seemed like it would take forever to get to this point and now twelve more hours seems longer than those two days. Were you able to reach your family? Have you called anyone? You haven't have you? Why not?" She pushed through tears.

"I will need my hand back to do that. You didn't talk long to him." I asked about her husband. "Is everything okay?"

Angelica held my hand tighter, kissed it and said. "He didn't have much to say to me. I didn't have much to say to him either. Truthfully, I have been thinking about someone else this whole time. Someone else has had my heart. I need to go back to my cabin and get some rest. It looks like we will have at least one more long night together and it feels like an eternity to me." She hugged me tight in her arms, putting no space between her heart and mine. "There's something I want to tell you." Angelica whispered in my ear and held me a few seconds longer. "Happy Valentine's Day."

She held me in her arms. She didn't want to go, I didn't want to go but we couldn't stay.

8pm

Angelica was right. We were both overwhelmed and exhausted. News of our salvation was salted by a week of hunger, thirst, pissing in bottles, shitting in bags, no baths and no sleep all in the stench of a dead ship.

"Cabin 83-74." I said to myself. "May this be the last time I cross your threshold." I laid in the doorway again and listened to my neighbors move around, pack and bring their luggage to the hallway. I was already packed, just the same as I came on board with the exception of a duffle bagged filled with alcohol. The exhaustion caught up to me and for two hours I closed my eyes and listened to Mahler.

I was awakened by the sound of the Triumph's horn as we approached the harbor. The blast was followed by cheers coming from within the ship and from the dock. I took the short walk down the hallway again, up the stairs and out deck 10. Several hundred passengers crowded the railings on the port side of the ship. Thousands of people stood anxiously on the dock waiting for the Triumph to come to a stop.

Some of the crew came out to the railing. They had never made port in Mobile Alabama and were excited to see a new city.

Two young women, crew members from Thailand totting small pals and plastic gloves stood next to me and one said. "What's it like in Mobile Alabama. Do they like to party here, because I think we're going to be here for awhile. Are you going to stay in Mobile, because we could use like a connection if you know what I mean."

"I don't think Mobile Alabama is your type of party town. The very last slave ship to come to the United States came here. Many of my ancestors came in through here and into the plantations of the South. It has a long history, but it is not as big or rich as Houston. So their club scene might be a little different." I told them.

"You mean it's ghetto! Woohoo! We like it like that!" The girls clapped their hands together and watched as more people crowded the dock and station below. "I don't know what the big deal is though. I mean, I spent four weeks on the river in a tiny cramped boat with no power to get out of my country. This was much better than that. Well, you're almost home and I hope you got a chance to do everything you wanted." The girls moved on pretending to wipe down the railings. We were still moving, but slower than before. I was so close that I felt comforted this nightmare was almost over. Until..

"Ding, ding, ding."

It was Jen. "Good evening to everyone, rather good night and as you can see we have arrived at our destination in Mobile Alabama. We have run into a little snag that's going to hold up our disembarkation process for just a few more minutes. Apparently there is a locomotive on the tracks that has to clear first. Of all things once the train clears the track we can continue. This kind of thing would never have happened in London."

"Ding."

What I would give for two Scots.

I had not finished listening to the end of Mahler's Symphony number one, so I picked it up right in the middle of the fourth movement right where Angelica I left it the night before. It was this triumphant return that brought us into the harbor as thousands of people on the dock cheered our arrival.

The Triumph sounded its horn.

Our captors devised an orderly surrender of the ship by deck in which meant I would be one of the last to leave. A sudden rush came over me as I realized I didn't know Angelica's last name, I didn't know her address, I didn't have her phone number, I didn't even have her email address. I had no way to contact her.

I had to find her before we left the ship!

Deck 5 was the holding area for the upper deck's disembarkation. The crew got the band together and played in the walkway as passengers came through. I took a seat deep in the middle of the darkened casino area and watched as passengers from the other decks passed.

Most of the lower decks were gone. Deck five was leaving and deck six, Angelica's deck, was on the way. Deck six passed. Deck seven came and went.

My heart sank. I wondered where Angelica was. I worried and feared that I would never see her again. I felt impaled through my chest and my soul ached at the possibility of not seeing her again. All I wanted was to just see her one more time. I needed that in my life. We spent every minute of the past week together at the bar just around the corner or on the rails of deck 10 and dreamed of how our life would be and where we would go. When there was nothing else we had each other. All I wanted was her. I could feel the darkness of the ship closing in around me. I was afraid of what my life would be like without her and now she was gone and I'd never see her again. She left without a good bye. She left me there alone and by myself. I was back where I started.

I was angry and hurt and as they called deck 8. I didn't want to live the ship. I wanted to stay there in the misery and in the darkness. I could see that car coming up the street, the devil's ride, and I felt its lights against my back. I felt the powerless urge to give into my depression. Until..

I was near broken when Angelica came back to the bar across from the casino. She looked around for me searching the crowd as droves of people strolled by. She watched the lines of deck 8 carefully once from front to back and again twice over. She couldn't see me sitting in the darkness of the ship so she went back to the bar and asked the bartender if he had seen me. He said no. She searched the lines again and went back to the bar and waited.

Crying and sobbing I grabbed my bags together ready to run over to her and make plans to see each other again.

I stood up and couldn't move. As suddenly as the pressure from my heart pumped to my feet and to my head, I looked around and was in a new place. I felt her love radiate across the room and warm my body. There was no car. There were no lights. There was no more fear. There was no more hunger. There was no anger. She came back for me. There was no depression. I mattered to someone. I was stronger.

Angelica was right and we needed to be strong for each other and that meant me being able to see my triggers for depression before they took hold of me. Her strength made me stronger. And now I needed to be strong for her, so I didn't move and watched her as she waited and looked for me.

Angelica waited until all of deck 8 was gone and finally she smiled, tapped her finger against the bar and left.

I never saw or spoke to her again.

"Thank you Angelica, I love you." I pushed through tears. I was stronger now, stronger than I had ever been. Seeing the depression within me wasn't enough to let it go, I also needed Angelica's to walk me through it. There was nothing more I could ask of her.

As deck 9 came down I stepped out of the shadows and into the light confident, assured, strong and exclaimed.

"La commedia è finita!"

Friday, February 15, 2013

Home

12:02 am

The line from the Triumph to the buses moved quickly so I only spent a few minutes in the dock area before boarding a bus headed for New Orleans. I arrived at the New Orleans Hilton Riverside at 2:30 am and was given a room to myself on the 14 floor. Once there I submerged myself into the tub for three hours. The sensation of hot water singed my chest and burned away the thick film across my skin and eyes. After the bath I ate several dinners the hotel provided for us. I was hungry again, but this time for the right reasons. Afterwards I took another bath and finally after more then six days awake, I fell asleep taking a long nap.

That afternoon I was given a taxi to the airport, while there I walked around the concourse and soaked in normal life. People where patiently waiting in line, buying snacks, smiling, laughing and eating. They enjoyed the restaurants, but I still couldn't breathe. A man threw a half empty bottle of water in the trash and walked by me as though it was nothing. I was changed forever.

I took a flight out of New Orleans to Hobby airport and landed in Houston Friday night. The high altitude helped drain my sinuses and popped my ears. I wondered where Angelica was and how she doing. The circle was complete and by 9:30 pm I was on my porch.

I walked in and remembered telling Angelica about my home; I walked her through the front door and took her through every room. She was with me in my heart and has been every day since. I was home.

Wednesday April 3, 2013

The Triumph while docked at the Mobile Alabama port for repairs breaks loose under hurricane force winds. The dock is destroyed and one person is killed.

Special thanks and remembrances to my friends who often crowded the rear bar of Club Rio on deck 5 in search of a dwindling supply of power, optimism, fresh water and smiles:

The Aggie Lawyer "The Advocate", thanks for all the stimulating conversation.

"Dutch" for organizing and manning the power bar and always staying civil about it.

The "Sistas" from Houston, staying beautiful and graceful during harsh times.

"Young Orson Welles" a student at the University of Houston, what a wonderful tale in poetry about our experience."

"Q- Tarantino" for taking the time to get personal on camera interviews preserving our experience and allowing everyone to have a voice and be remembered, and everyone else who came by and lent a hand and a story.

Finally, special thanks to my steward who never left his post, always watching the opened prison cell doors of the port side aft section of deck 8 and for a small price could find the last bottle of water on the ship and a can of air freshener. Thank you.

The February Triumph